LEGENDS OF

Takiwa-waiariki — the land of the Hot Springs

LEGENDS OF ROTORUA

by
A. W. REED

with illustrations by
DENNIS TURNER

REED

This book is a facsimile edition of a book published in 1958, reprinted by popular request. The language and illustrations reflect the attitudes of the time.

Published by Reed Books, a division of Reed Publishing (NZ) Ltd, 39 Rawene Rd, Birkenhead, Auckland. Associated companies, branches and representatives throughout the world.

This book is copyright. Except for the purpose of fair reviewing, no part of this publication may be reproduced or transmitted in any form or by any means, electronic or mechanical, including photocopying, recording, or any information storage and retrieval system, without permission in writing from the publisher. Infringers of copyright render themselves liable to prosecution.

ISBN 0 7900 0566 2

Text © 1958 A.W. Reed
Illustrations © 1958 Dennis Turner

The author and illustrator assert their moral rights in the work.

First published 1958
Reprinted 1997

Printed in New Zealand
Printed in Australia
Printed in Hong Kong
Printed in Singapore

CONTENTS

1	Ngatoro the Fire-Bringer	page 9
2	Ihenga the Name-Giver	16
3	Ohinemutu	20
4	Rotorua Township	28
5	Whakarewarewa	35
6	Lake Rotorua	43
7	Mokoia Island	53
8	Lake-side Villages and Springs Te Ngae: Mourea: Hamurana Springs: Taniwha Springs: Fairy Springs	67
9	Ngongotaha	81
10	Tikitere	87
11	Rotoiti and Hongi's Track	92
12	The Eastern Lakes Rotoehu and Rotoma: Okataina	105
13	The Story of Hatupatu	110
14	The Blue and Green Lakes Lake Tikitapu: Lake Rotokakahi	128
15	Tarawera and the Eruption Te Wairoa — The Buried Village: Tarawera: Rotomahana	136
16	Place Names of the Thermal Region	145

ILLUSTRATIONS

Takiwa-waiariki — the land of the Hot Springs	*Frontispiece*
Ngatoro throws his slave into the crater of Ngauruhoe	*page* 12
The steam of Karapiti pointed to Maketu	14
Ihenga and his men survey the new land of lakes and geysers	18
Ihenga laments for his daughter	22
The cursing of Ruapeka pa	25
Tukutuku and Papakino danced in the darkness	26
The battle of "the waters of jumping whitebait"	30
The storehouse made from Hatupatu's cloak	33
The war-dance of the army of Wahiao	37
Waikite—the water seen from afar	38
The Brainpot at Whakarewarewa	39
Pohutu geyser by moonlight	40
The Papakura geyser and the Puarenga Stream	41
Ihenga carries off the posts from the village of Tu-o-Rotorua	45
Hatupatu dives down to the bed of Lake Rotorua	48
Taoi poises for the dive	51
The kumara god of Mokoia Island	55
The warning of the gulls	58
Tutanekai finds his lover	64
Flying Cloud's canoe overwhelms the defenders of Mokoia Island	71
Hamurana Springs, the home of Hinerua	73
The capture of the taniwha of the Dark Chasm	77
The pool where the gods once played	79
Ihenga throws his torch into the bracken	82

ILLUSTRATIONS

Ihenga flees from the fairy people of Ngongotaha	85
The greatly loved daughter of Tikitere	88
The lake of the shags	90
The assault on Kakanui	95
The bones of Tutea are taken to the cave below the falls	97
Onguru, the place of testing of canoes	99
Hinehopu's Wishing Tree	101
Hongi's warriors drag their canoes across the portage	102
Kotiora and his young wife	107
The laughter of Te Rangi-takaroro	109
The rock where Hatupatu hid from the ogress	114
The death of the bird-woman	116
Hatupatu comes out of his hiding place to face his brothers	119
Hatupatu's army of warriors	122
The gift of the head of Raumati	124
The tohungas chant a karakia to overcome the taniwha	130
The search for the lost tiki of the Blue Lake	132
The island of Motutawa	134
The overwhelming of Te Wairoa	138
The burial of Tuhourangi	140
The phantom canoe of Lake Tarawera	142
The Little islands in Lake Rotomahana	144
Baptism scene	158
Te Toto, "the Place of Blood", now Picnic Point	160

FOREWORD

Rotorua is a land of romance. Every hill and valley, every geyser and boiling mud pool, every lake and island and indentation of the shore — every one was known by name and loved by the Maori people. Many of these places were remembered in fable and story, and this is not surprising. A region of violent thermal activity is an obvious setting for tales of mystery and magic, many of which have been handed down from the distant past.

These tales come to us from the unwritten records of a cultured race. Because of the pioneer work done in the field of research by Sir George Grey, and in later years by Mr James Cowan, we have written records of many of these fabulous stories. Their work has been drawn upon extensively for this book, but further information has come from several other sources.

Grateful acknowledgement is made to Mr Dennis Turner for the perceptive drawings which illustrate these tales. Whatever may be the merit of this book, at least it has some claim on the attention of the reader as a collection of drawings by an outstanding interpreter of Maori life and customs. I should also like to express my gratitude to Mr J. H. Richards and to Mr J. M. Reed for help with the text and layout.

A. W. Reed

Wellington,
September 1958

Chapter One

NGATORO THE FIRE-BRINGER

TE ARAWA IS THE CANOE. Proud vanguard of the Fleet, it sailed southward from Tahiti six centuries ago. Its crew settled at Maketu in the Bay of Plenty and spread inland. Today the Arawa people live in the Hot Lakes district, the guardians of the weird thermal region of New Zealand.

The right to their ancestral lands came from occupation, and from the early wanderings of Ngatoro-i-rangi, the famous tohunga of the *Arawa* canoe. It was Ngatoro who found dry valleys, and stamped his foot so that springs of water gushed forth. It was Ngatoro who first visited the mountains and placed on them the mysterious white-skinned fairy people, the patu-paiarehe. It was Ngatoro who was the cause of volcanic fire, spouting geysers and boiling mud pools.

This is the story of how fire came to the thermal regions. Leaving his home at Maketu, Ngatoro travelled southwards until he reached the great plain to the east of Lake Taupo. As he rested there, the clouds rolled away and he saw the shining majesty of Mount Tongariro, and his heart was filled with longing to ascend the virgin peak. He called his companions and they travelled south until they reached the place where the land swelled upwards.

"Stay here," Ngatoro commanded his followers. "I will climb to the top of the mountain, but none of you may come with me except the slave Auruhoe. This is a hazardous venture and if I am to return in safety you who remain behind must heed my words. While I am gone, you may eat no food. This will give me strength and the gods will be with me. When I return we will feast together and I will tell you of the things that I learn from that mountain."

Ngatoro and the slave Auruhoe walked quickly, passing from the bush and the loud singing of birds to the stillness of the mountainside and the white never-ending snow. His step was shortened in the yielding snow of the steep slope. The breath of the two men hung in the air as a white cloud, and biting cold numbed their faces and hands and feet. Auruhoe fell, but Ngatoro urged him on.

"If it were easy to come this way there would be no purpose," he said.

Auruhoe paid little heed. The cold had frozen hands and feet and clutched his heart with icy fingers. He stumbled after Ngatoro. The sun was hidden and clouds drifted over the summit. Their feet moved slowly and in the vast silence the cold wrapped their bodies and crept through flesh and bone, until they felt brittle, like dry sticks.

A few more paces and Ngatoro and his slave fell forward on their faces, for the steep walls had given way to the sharp pointed summit.

In the warm, green valley far below, Ngatoro's followers had waited long.

"Perhaps he has perished," one of them said. "We may wait long for them, and hunger is an impatient thing. Let us eat."

With sidelong glances at the mountain, they had lit their cooking fires. There were no clouds on the mountain and in the bright snow the figures of Ngatoro and Auruhoe had dwindled to nothing. But as they ate, the cold drove its icy fingers deep towards the tohunga's heart.

In his agony he prayed to his sisters in Hawaiki. "Send fire to warm me," he called. "Do not delay or I shall perish. O Kuiwai and Haungaroa! come quickly. *Ka riro au i te tonga!*"* (I am carried away in the cold south wind.)

In far-off Hawaiki his sisters heard his prayer. They called the fire demons, Te Pupu and Te Hoata, who plunged into the sea and swam quickly past the throat of Te Parata, the dreaded sea-monster, until they came to Whakaari, or White Island, as the pakeha has named the island inferno of the Bay of Plenty. As they lifted their heads into the air the earth burst into flames which have never died down. They found they still had many miles to go before reaching Ngatoro. Below the sea once more the bubbling, steaming wake showed the path of the fire demons. At Mou-tohora they surfaced momentarily, and again at Okakaru, Rotoehu, Rotoiti, Rotorua, Tarawera, Orakei-Korako and Taupo. At each place the flames roared through the orifices. The tunnel they made was supposed by the Maoris to connect Tongariro with White Island ever after.

Like a flash of lightning the fire demons sped through

*It is from *riro*, carried away, and *tonga*, south wind, that Tongariro has received its name, which was originally applied to the three peaks, Tongariro, Ngauruhoe and Ruapehu.

Ngatoro throws his slave into the crater of Ngauruhoe

the enormous pyramid of Tongariro, bursting from the summit as Ngatoro lay in the extremity of death. His slave had already succumbed to the intense cold, but in the fierce volcanic heat Ngatoro revived. The warm blood crept through his veins and strength flowed into his arms and legs. As the flames danced on the snow, turning it blood-red, and the dense smoke swathed his body, the priest picked up the body of Auruhoe, his slave, and cast it into the crater, which has ever since been known as Ngauruhoe.

So it was, the old men say, that the fire demons raged underground and came up at Rotorua and other places in their search for Ngatoro-i-rangi. It was because of the great tohunga of the Arawa canoe, who dared to ascend the mountain for his people, that the fire gods play under the thin crust of earth in the wonderland of New Zealand.

There is a legend of Ngati-Tuwharetoa which links the story of Ngatoro and the fire-gods with the taniwha of Taupo. This tale has been told by Mr John Grace and is now related with his permission:

Kuiwai was a younger sister of Ngatoro-i-rangi and she lived in Hawaiki. She was married to a chief called Manaia.

One day the husband ill-treated Kuiwai and, with her sister Haungaroa and a man named Tanewhakaraka and two servants, she left for Aotearoa.* The party landed on the Hawke's Bay coast, and from a place called Tawhiu-whiu journeyed across the Kaingaroa Plains to Maketu in the Bay of Plenty where Ngatoro-i-rangi had established his home.

During their journey across the plains they came to a place called Waiwhakaari by Mount Tauhara, close to the northern shores of Lake Taupo. They had expected to find Ngatoro-i-rangi temporarily at Taupo, as it was from

---

*The ancient name of New Zealand.

The steam of Karapiti pointed to Maketu

Tongariro's peak that he appealed to fire to save him from freezing to death. However, they discovered that he had left the district.

One of the gods that Ngatoro-i-rangi brought from Hawaiki was Horomatangi. It came to this god's notice that Kuiwai and her sister were in the vicinity of Tauhara mountain so he decided he would go to Taupo to direct them to the Bay of Plenty. He dived into the sea off White Island and, travelling underground, emerged from Lake Taupo. As he came to the surface he blew pumice and water high into the air.

From above the lake he saw Kuiwai and her party in the distance. He dived back into the lake and as he entered his underground channel a great whirlpool was formed at the entrance. The channel which it formed exists today and is situated about two miles north-east of Motutaiko Island and at the bottom of Horomatangi reef.

In order to advise Kuiwai and her sister where Ngatoro-i-rangi was to be found, he went back into his tunnel and exhaled his breath with such force that he caused the Karapiti blowhole at Wairakei. The white steam rose straight and high into the heavens and then turned in the direction of Maketu. Kuiwai observed this and knew where to find Ngatoro-i-rangi.

Horomatangi thereafter lived in his hole off Motutaiko. At times he is said to assume the form of a lizard. As such he is known as Ihumataotao. In the lake he takes the form of a black rock.

Chapter Two

IHENGA THE NAME-GIVER

THE MEN OF *Te Arawa*, the canoe of the Great Fleet in the long ago, made their sacred places and established a right to their lands. Tama-te-kapua, captain of *Te Arawa*, died and was buried on the windy heights of Moehau on the Coromandel Peninsula. The body of his son, Tuhoro, was later laid to rest in the same place by his son, Ihenga. "When I am buried," Tuhoro had said, "go to Maketu."

Ihenga journeyed south to Maketu, the landing place of *Te Arawa*, where he was greeted by his uncle, Kahumata-momoe. From Maketu Ihenga set off on a hunting expedition with his friends, taking his dog, Potaka-tawhiti, with him.

They crossed swamps and hills, until they came to a place where kiwis were found. It was the late afternoon but many birds were caught. Ihenga and his companions sat down to rest. Potaka went on alone, chasing one of the birds through the dense bush. The kiwi ran down-

IHENGA THE NAME-GIVER

hill until it came to the shores of a lake, where it tried to escape by running into the water. Potaka pounced on it and killed it, and then began to drink the fresh water, at the same time swallowing mouthfuls of inanga, or whitebait, which were swarming in the shallow water.

When his thirst was satisfied Potaka picked the kiwi up in his mouth and returned to his master.

"Ho, the dog has found water," Ihenga said when he saw Potaka's dripping coat. "Perhaps there is a lake somewhere below."

He was anxious to go on, but his friends had already lit the cooking fires. "He has probably found a stream," they said. After a while Potaka began to roll on the ground, for his fish meal was not agreeing with him. He lay full length and disgorged the fish.

"See, it must be a lake," Ihenga said excitedly. "Let us find it before the night comes on."

Leaving the food to cook itself in the earth oven, the hunters followed Potaka, who ran in front, barking and frisking through the ferns. Presently they broke through the last of the trees and found the little lake shining in the rays of the setting sun. Shoals of inanga were still leaping in the water close to the beach. The hunters gathered fern fronds and wove them into a primitive net, with which they caught many fish. Some they ate, and the rest they took back with them to Maketu the next day.

"These are the fish we caught in a lake far over the hills," Ihenga said to Kahu. "It belongs to me and my children for ever, for I have named it Te-roto-iti-kite-a-Ihenga" (The little lake seen by Ihenga). Lake Rotoiti was the first place discovered and named by Ihenga.

Some time later a boy was born to him, and when he was able to run about with the other children, Kahu said to Ihenga:

Ihenga and his men survey the new land of lakes and geysers

IHENGA THE NAME-GIVER

"You have found one little lake. The time has come now for you to go far over the land and claim it for your children."

Taking four men with him, Ihenga set out on the famous journey in which he claimed land for his child and for all the people of *Te Arawa* for all time.

They climbed the long ridge and looked back with affection to their home at Maketu. From the crest of the hill they could see far across the land. Ihenga surveyed the country, which looked fair and promising, and then his face fell. "See, there are others before us. There is the smoke of their fire." He did not know then that all they had seen was steam wafted from a hot spring.

The five explorers entered the forest and went on until they came to a waterfall and then to a lake which was larger than the little lake which he had seen on his earlier expedition, and this lake, it is believed, he named Roto-rua-nui-a-Kahu (Second and big lake of Kahu).

The island in the lake he called Te motu-tapu-a-Tinirau (The sacred island of Tinirau), which was a name of olden time. It was later named Mokoia and is known as Mokoia to this day. On the shores of Lake Rotorua, Ihenga pitted his wits against the chief Tu-o-Rotorua, as we shall see in Chapter 6.

Ihenga, who travelled far through the northland as well as in the thermal regions, was the great name-giver of the Arawa tribal lands, and Kahu-mata-momoe, his uncle, was second only to him.

We shall meet them both again as we read the old-time legends of the mysterious land of the hot lakes.

Chapter Three

OHINEMUTU

THE HEALING SPRINGS of Rotorua have been spoken of as Wai-ora-a-Tane (Living water of Tane), in which the moon bathes each month in the great lake of Aewa. The moon dies, the Maori says, but in those living waters she receives the gift of life to sustain her in her passage through the heavens. The township of Rotorua with its ngawha, or hot springs, has provided living waters for many thousands of sufferers. Takiwa-waiariki is the old-time Maori name for the hot springs district, and it is in the town of Rotorua, and especially in the Government Spa, that Nature's healing waters are mainly located.

The first township was at Ohinemutu, the Maori settlement where Ihenga, grandson of Tama-te-kapua, settled with his people more than five centuries ago. He had one daughter, Kakara, whom he loved greatly. This girl, the sweet-scented one, was killed by the people who lived at

Owhata on the eastern shore of the lake. When news of her death was brought to Ihenga, he went down to the water's edge and sang his lament or tangi:

E hine e! Ka mutu nei ano taku tamahine i te ao, ko Kakara! (Alas, girl! You are severed for ever from this world, my daughter, Kakara.)

The lament of the broken-hearted father was made as he stood on a flat rock close to the place where the little Anglican Church of St. Faith's now stands among the eerie steam vents of the foreshore. This rock in the shallow waters of the lake was the tino, the essential spirit, of Ohinemutu (Place of the girl cut off). It received its name from the words hine (girl) and mutu (cut off or ended) with the prefix "O", which almost invariably means "the place of" in Maori nomenclature. In the course of time the name was given to the pa.

Gilbert Mair, who lived for many years amongst the Arawa people, said that Ihenga set up a stone in memory of his daughter as a rahui (a mark to warn people against trespassing) "to punish the murderers" and to keep their crime fresh in the memory of his people. The stone, which was about three feet high and painted red, was preserved and venerated for several centuries, but it disappeared in the 1880s.

There can surely be few stranger villages than the old Maori pa of Ohinemutu, tucked away on the steaming shore of Ruapeka Bay and on the peninsula of Muruika. Lieutenant Meade, who visited the village in 1863 and was entertained by Captain Mair, referred to the inhabitants living in a perpetual cloud of steam. "The whole village," he wrote, "is built on a thin crust of rock and soil, roofing over one vast boiler. Hot springs hiss and seethe in every direction, some spouting upwards and boiling with the greatest fury, others merely at an agreeable warmth. From

Ihenga laments for his daughter

every crack and crevice spurt forth jets of steam or hot air, and the open bay of the lake itself is studded far and near with boiling springs and bubbling steam-jets. So thin is the crust on which men have built their little town and lived for generations, that in most places after merely thrusting a walking-stick into the ground beneath our feet, steam instantly followed its withdrawal."

There is an old-time story which links Ohinemutu with Rotoaira, the little lake which nestles between Tongariro and Pihanga to the south of Lake Taupo. Hurukareao, a water monster or dragon, lived in this lake and had taken under its protection the hapu, or sub-tribe, which lived in the pa by the lakeside. The inhabitants of the pa were so blameless in their lives that when Horomatangi,* a relative

*See the earlier adventures of Horomatangi in Chapter One.

of Hurukareao, who lived in Lake Taupo, sought for a tribe which enjoyed a similar reputation, he could find none to equal them. The two taniwhas agreed to take the same hapu at Rotoaira under their care.

Amongst the people at Rotoaira was a young woman of adventurous disposition named Hine-utu. Having heard of the reputation of the hot springs at Ohinemutu, she travelled north and stayed there for a short time. The Arawa people held Hine-utu in little esteem, and unfortunately they had not heard of the favour in which her tribe were held by the taniwha of Taupo and Rotoaira. Hine-utu was teased and tormented by the young people. Incensed, she hurried back to her home and called for revenge from Hurukareao and his cousin. Her incantations roused the taniwhas to such indignation that they threw their enormous bodies about in the water, with disastrous results. Great waves engulfed the pa at Rotoaira. At Tokaanu the surging waters changed the channel of the river and submerged the pa on its banks. Through the lake and over the hills the two taniwhas sped northward on their mission of vengeance. Eventually they reached Ohinemutu, but the journey had wearied them, and although the waters mounted over the village, only half of it was submerged and many of the inhabitants escaped.

If proof of this legend is needed, for proof is so often required by the unimaginative pakeha, it is said that there are three springs, one at Rotoaira, one at Tokaanu and another at Ohinemutu, all of which are named Hurukareao. And on the island of Motutaiko, in Lake Taupo, Horomatangi still lives in an underwater cave. For many years he upset passing canoes and devoured their crews. Nowadays he lies deep in the cave and snaps harmlessly at the propellers of the launches, the taniwhas whose power has outmatched his own.

For many years the pakeha has agreed that the carved totara posts at the lake-edge of Muruika Point are the remains of a submerged village, but the Ngati-Whakaue people will have nothing to do with the versions of southern tribes, in spite of their claims to perfection and protection of powerful taniwha.

It is six generations since the Muruika pa, sometimes known as Ruapeka pa, sank into the lake with the loss of all but two of its inhabitants. No doubt the gods who preside over the internal fires dragged it down from the land of daylight, but there are several versions to account for the disaster. The forces of fire and volcanic destruction were unleashed, some say by the agency of high-born Te Rangi-puriti, father of Tuhoto Ariki, who was believed to have some mysterious connection with the eruption of Mount Tarawera in 1886; others say that the pa was cursed by Te Ara-tukutuku, a woman of great mana, in revenge for another arising.

A last account relates the story of two evil-minded priestesses named Tukutuku and Papakino who quarrelled with the people of Ohinemutu. Wildly they danced before the tuahu (the tribe's sacred place), obscene and frightening in the dark night, until lightning flashed down from a clear sky and the fire god erupted through the shallow waters of the lake, engulfing the pa and all its inhabitants. Tukutuku and Papakino were caught up in the disaster of their own making, and now they lie beneath the water a few hundred yards from Muruika Point, turned to stone. You may see their forms beneath the shallow water as you drift over them in a dinghy, and remember the malignancy of that black night so many years ago.

In the modern village several buildings cluster round the marae or square of Papaiouru. On the lakeside, on Muruika Point, is the Church of St. Faith's. The mission

The cursing of Ruapeka pa

hall is called Te Aomarama (The World of Light), but the old gods still make their presence felt. The carved meeting house, Tama-te-kapua, stands on the southern side of the marae, named after "The son of the clouds", who was the captain of the *Arawa* canoe on its journey to Aotearoa. Although the great navigator's resting-place is on the windy heights of Coromandel Peninsula, his descendants have spread inland from Maketu through the thermal country and his name is ever-green in their memory.

The power of the ancient gods is not easily cancelled. Strong tapu lay over the bay of Ruapeka and on the shore — so strong that no one dared make room for a Christian church to be built until, in the year 1884, the

Tukutuku and Papakino danced in the darkness

Ngati-Whakaue of Ohinemutu sent for the dreaded Tuhoto of Te Wairoa. By incantation and karakia he drew the tapu away from the settlement until it lay heavily on one tiny islet close to the shore. This was hardly more than a rock crowned by a single flax bush, but it was dignified by the name Te Motutapu, the sacred island. The powers of darkness were confined to the little island and the solitary flax bush which few dared approach. It was in the shade of this flax bush, long ago, that the heads of chiefs who had been killed in battles were smoked and preserved. This in itself would make the island tapu. On a sunny day it is hard to imagine that such silent power is pressing on the leaves of the flax bush of Te Motutapu, but the ancient gods are waiting.

CHAPTER FOUR

ROTORUA TOWNSHIP

TAKE THE HEART-LEAF OF A FLAX BUSH — any except the tapu bush on the little island in the bay of Ruapeka — fashion it into the shape of a canoe, place a pebble in it to represent yourself, and launch it on the waters of the lake. The gentle south wind will carry it to the girl of your dreams and turn her thoughts to you:

I launch, O Hiri, my little flax-boat;
Beautiful are you, O most desirable love.

Songs and dances, chants and incantations were the very life of the Maori, and song is still the natural expression of this warm-hearted people. James Cowan has told us of the girl, sighing for her absent lover, sitting on Pukeroa Hill, once the very centre of Ngati-Whakaue life. The village was strongly fortified, and there were cultivations of kumara and taro where the football ground has been made in Pukeroa Park. It is a song which links the old and the new, as the Maori girl looks down on the busy township and over the quiet waters of Lake Rotorua and sings:

> *He kainga hikareti noku ki Pukeroa;*
> *Mokemoke te rere a te auahi, e te tau!*

> Here I sit, smoking my cigarette
>   On Pukeroa Hill;
> Lonely drifts the smoke away,
>   O love of mine!

Pukeroa, the pa, and Ohinemutu, the kainga,* were the centres of Maori activity in Rotorua. The modern town was first laid out in 1881, its streets being named after famous Maori ancestors. The old kumara plantation Tiritiri-matangi, was in present-day Arawa Street, where the post office stands. Its name conjures up a peaceful scene which is in striking contrast with the busy street. Tiritiri was the name given to the twigs which marked each kumara mound. The heaps were placed where they faced the sunshine and matangi, the north-east breeze.

The site of the Government Spa was an important place to the pre-pakeha Maori. Oruawhata was the old-time name of a deep pit or chasm of cold water where the modern gardens are situated, but it was also applied to the larger area of the sanatorium grounds. In the days of internecine warfare the chasm served a useful purpose, for the bones of Arawa chiefs were thrown into the pit, where they were safe from raiders who might otherwise have desecrated them by turning them into musical instruments. In the deep pool they were thrown, *"kia ngaro tonutia,"* as Cowan, to whom we owe so many of these local stories of Rotorua, records. They were "utterly and forever concealed."

---

*The pa was a fortified village to which the people retreated in time of war; the kainga was the unfortified settlement, close to the cultivations.

The battle of "the waters of jumping whitebait"

"That old waro* has long ago been covered over or filled in, and the pakeha's artificial fountains play, and roses and pansies bloom over the graves of the forgotten Arawas. The actual spot, originally named Oruawhata, is between the Blue Bath and the Malfroy Geysers."

These geysers were manufactured by the engineer in charge of the Thermal Springs District in the eighties. Centuries ago the geysers of Oruawhata had become quiescent, and were merely hot pools. They were used to supply warm swimming baths, but the flow was sometimes insufficient. Malfroy injected cold water into the springs so that workmen could connect them with pipes embedded in concrete. By means of these connecting pipes and controlling valves, the temperature of the water is kept constant and the pools can be stirred into activity. It was a skilled and imaginative engineering feat, and the artificial geysers, which are a source of interest to visitors, have been given his name.

The other natural springs of Oruawhata have also been tamed and applied to medicinal use. One of the most famous is the Priest's Bath, which was known to the Maori as Te Pupunitanga, or The Ambush. A story lies behind the name. Many hundreds of years ago a pet lizard belonging to a chief who lived beside lake Tikitapu was killed by a tribe called "the descendants of Tama of the albatross nose". Infuriated at the loss of the pet lizard, the people of Tikitapu lay in wait for their enemy in the manuka by the spring which was afterwards known as Te Pupunitanga. A fierce fight ensued. It was such a grim battle that it was called "the waters of jumping whitebait". It is said that the ground was covered with heaps of wounded men who twisted and writhed in agony so that

*Pit.

they resembled whitebait fighting to escape as the net is drawn ashore.

About 1865, long before there was a township at Rotorua, Father Mahoney, a Roman Catholic priest at Tauranga, who was crippled with rheumatism, heard of the healing waters of Te Pupunitanga. He walked slowly and painfully along the native tracks until he came to the medicinal spring and camped beside it. After a week of bathing in its healing waters he was completely cured. Such was the fame of this cure that the spring has since been known as the Priest's Bath.

The Maori had names for all these springs. Many were descriptive. The Rachel Bath was Whangapipiro, which refers to the strong smell of its sulphurous waters. The Postmaster Bath was Arikiroa (Long spring). The cloud of steam which rose when it was more active than at present was called Te Roro-o-te-rangi (The Brains of the Sky).

The Blue Bath, near the site of the fearsome chasm, may be said to be Oruawhata, a name which recalls one of the exploits of Hatupatu, more of whose story will be found in the chapter on Hatupatu. In this instance he divested himself of his flax cloak and hung it on the branches of a tree, thus making a store-house (whata) of it. He paused on the edge of the lake, dived in and swam underwater as far as Mokoia Island. It was in memory of this feat that a village on the marshy land by the lakeside, now deserted, was named Te Kauanga-a-Hatupatu (The Swimming of Hatupatu).

James Cowan collected a number of names of places in the grounds of the sanatorium which are reminders of grim battles or peaceful days of plenty before the coming of the white man. Picnic Point was Te Toto (The Blood, or "The Place of Blood"), a reminder of a particularly

The storehouse made from Hatupatu's cloak

fierce fight between two Arawa tribes. Close by, on a small island, was Te Ana-o-Waitapu (The Cave of Waitapu), where a chief of this name took refuge. Another place in the swampy ground near Picnic Point was Te Paepaehakumanu (The Place of Bird Snares), and still another, Tauhere-rau-ti (Bird snares of Cabbage-tree Leaves). The foreshore extending from the boundary of the sanatorium grounds to the wharf was Koura-mawhitiwhiti (Crayfish wriggling in the Net).

Te Papa-o-te-Arawa, The Rock of the Arawa, is the proud name borne by a long, flat rock near Picnic Point. Under the rock is a cave in which the bones of the dead were placed. It was a sacred place to the Maoris, and when the land was taken over by the pakeha, the bones were removed to another shrine.

Chapter Five

WHAKAREWAREWA

EVERY VISITOR TO ROTORUA is attracted by "Whaka", the region of intense thermal activity at the southern end of the town. "Whaka" it is for short, but this is an unfortunate contraction of the official name Whakarewarewa, and of the even more sonorous Te Whakarewarewatanga-o-te-ope-a-Wahiao. "Whaka", in the Maori language, is frequently used as the causative prefix to a word, denoting action and intensity.

This famous settlement, now occupied by descendants of the Tuhourangi tribe who left Te Wairoa, the Buried Village, at the time of the Tarawera Eruption in 1886, lies under Pohaturoa (Long Rock) and the lesser hills of Whakarewarewa and Te Puia. These heights were crowned by impregnable pas, or fortresses. It was the pa of Whakarewarewa which later gave its name to the larger area of geysers, boiling pools of water and mud, and sinter deposits.

There have been ingenious and fanciful interpretations of the name. In *The Hot Springs of New Zealand*, Herbert wrote that Rewa-rewa was mist or steam (a meaning not given by Williams's *Maori Dictionary*) and that whaka, as the causative, denoted the action of making the steam rise. Another local version of some ingenuity is one that compares the lace-like silicated sticks and leaves of the pools and geysers to the delicate inner bark of the rewarewa tree. But Williams records that Whakarewarewa means "a war-dance to make a show of force before attacking".

This brings us to the historical origin of the word as recorded by Cowan. Some two hundred and fifty years ago the chief Wahiao paraded his men at the foot of the hill before setting out on the warpath against another tribe. It was a large body of men, called an ope or army, and, as was customary, a war dance was performed before leaving. It must have been an impressive scene, as rank after rank leaped up from a kneeling position and the ground trembled with the thunderous stamping of feet and the deep-throated roar of the war chant. This was the leaping-up, the whakarewarewatanga, which was commemorated in the name afterwards given to the hilltop pa, Te Whakarewarewatanga-o-te-ope-o-Wahiao (The Leaping-up, the War Dance of the Army of Wahiao). The tribe which occupied the fortress was called Ngati-Wahiao after this ancestor.

The pa on the nearby hill was named, quite simply, Te Puia (The Geyser). The full imagery of the imaginative Maori people is shown in the names they gave to scores of solfataras, mud pools, steaming, effervescing cauldrons and geysers. The pakeha, who now refers to a mudpool with many concentric rings on its surface as the Gramophone Record Pool, cannot match the ingenuity of the Maoris

The war-dance of the army of Wahiao

Waikite—the water seen from afar

of a bygone day who named the thermal sights so picturesquely and imaginatively.

From time to time the thermal activity changes in intensity. Although it is now quiescent, the Waikite geyser was once the most commanding sight in the settlement. Because it could be seen from such a distance when it blossomed into eruption, it was known by the Maoris as Water seen from afar — Waikite. The pakeha contributed to the fancy, for at the suggestion of Captain Gilbert Mair and under the planning of S. Percy Smith, Fenton Street, two miles in length and straight as an arrow, pointed directly at the famous geyser.

Near the site of the now-quiet Waikite geyser is the Brain Pot. Unmistakable in shape, this cauldron is notable now only for its distinctive appearance, but long ago it

The Brainpot at Whakarewarewa

was also a geyser. Te Komutumutu (The Calabash with the Top cut off) is its Maori name. Some little distance away is the Tukutuku Cave, near the junction of two paths, and the alkaline spring, Te Hinau, is close by. It was in this cave that Te Tukutuku, an old Maori chief, hid for two years from his enemies. Eventually he was discovered and beheaded. His brains were cooked in the geyser which, because of its shape, was likened to a calabash. It preserves a memory of the grim story in its popular name, The Brainpot.

Pohutu, the most spectacular of the geysers of the present time, takes its name from the splashing which it makes. The Papakura geyser, in the south-west corner of the reserve, gave its name to Maggie Papakura, a famous guide, who was the mother-in-law of the no less famous Rangi.

Pohutu geyser by moonlight

As the tourist enters the reserve he passes under the War Memorial archway which guards the bridge across the stream, and then watches the children diving for coins in the warm waters of the Puarenga Stream, which meanders through the reserve after emerging from the Hemo Gorge. "Te Hokowhitu-a-Tu" (The Force of the War-god Tu), reads the inscription on the arched entrance to the thermal area. There is a curious mixture of ideas contained in the name of the stream, for the adjective puarenga means muddy, and it is true that the water is heavily discoloured. If the word is broken up into its component parts we have pua, meaning flower, and renga, which has many meanings, and among them, overflowing, discoloured, yellow or, as a noun, the pollen of the native reed or raupo. It has been suggested that pua-renga is a reference to the flowers of

The Papakura geyser and the Puarenga Stream

sulphur, which are like the pollen of the raupo, floating on the surface of the water.

Visitors are always taken to Rotowhio Model Pa, which is built on the site of an old fighting pa, and takes its name from a little lake, which can be seen nearby. The picturesque name Rotowhio means Lake of the Blue Duck.

On the north side of the Taupo Road, and on the edge of the golf-links, is the mysterious no-man's-land, Arikikapakapa — the fluttering or flapping hot springs. Kapakapa is usually descriptive of the flapping of a bird's wings or the fluttering of hands in the haka, the native dance, and is a good descriptive word for the noise made by the plopping mud pools. Waimangeao Creek, which drains Arikikapakapa Lake, means Pungent Waters, and is known to the pakeha as Alum Creek. It runs through the Papangaeheehe (Rocky

Flat of rustling Sounds) and tumbles down the Rumbling Waters (Waiharuru Fall) in the sulphurous area known to the pakeha as Sodom and Gomorrah.

Chapter Six

LAKE ROTORUA

VISITORS TO THE HOT LAKES quickly discover that Roto, which appears so often on the map, means lake. It makes a curious but unavoidable redundancy, for Rotorua the town must be differentiated from Rotorua the lake. Rua is a name with many meanings, and of these Bishop Selwyn, an early visitor to the lake, guessed that it was used in the sense of "two", supported by the fact that Rotorua and Rotoiti, joined by the Ohau Channel, really form a double lake. "The lakes," he wrote, "which have caused the name Rotorua . . . are joined together by a small stream like a chain-shot."

The true explanation of the name is equally simple. Ihenga, whom we have met earlier, came a second time to Rotoiti, and then went on to Rotorua, which he named the "Second Lake". The name in full was Rotorua-nui-a-Kahu (Second and big Lake of Kahu).

When the famous chief arrived at the lake, he played a

trick to serve his own ends. He could not be sure that he was the first arrival at the lake, for the steam rising from Ohinemutu had the appearance of cooking fires. He assured himself that there was no one there, but when he came to the crest of a hill and looked down he saw the village of Waiohiro, by Utuhina, the Ohinemutu stream, and a fire burning there. Close by there was a net hanging from a food-platform. He went down stealthily and searched until he found the tuahu or sacred place of the village. There was no one about at the time. He carried away the posts, a pile of decaying whitebait, and even some of the earth, and used them to set up a tuahu of his own at the foot of the hill Kawaha. The posts were old and partly burnt.

Then he took new posts and set them up in fresh earth at the place where the fire was burning, and hung newly-stripped bark and green flax on the posts. Back at Kawaha he conducted a little ceremony of his own and named his tuahu Te Pera-o-Tangaroa. By the time he had finished, the people of the village were returning. Ihenga swung his cloak round his shoulders and went to meet them.

The folk of the village saw him coming and waved to him. Their chief, whose name was Tu-o-Rotorua, greeted him and asked if he had just arrived.

"Ho! This is my land," Ihenga replied truculently.

Tu-o-Rotorua looked puzzled. "I mean, where do you live?"

"This is my very own land."

"But, as you can see, we have been living here for a long time."

"No," Ihenga said firmly, "you have come after me. The land is mine by right of discovery."

Tu-o-Rotorua's face hardened. "What sign can you show to prove that the land is yours?"

"What sign have you?" Ihenga asked.

Ihenga carries off the posts from the village of Tu-o-Rotorua

Tu-o-Rotorua smiled grimly. "You shall see for yourself. It is a tuahu, which will surely establish my right to this land."

"Very well. By the tuahu shall proof be made. Show it to me, but know that I too have a tuahu. If it is clear that your tuahu is older than mine, then it will be a sign that the land is yours by right of occupation."

They went together to the tuahu, followed by the other people. Tu-o-Rotorua said nothing, but his eyes widened as he saw the newly-cut posts, the raw earth and the freshly pulled bark and flax. There was a puzzled look in his eyes as he followed Ihenga back to the post of Kawaha. When they came to Te Pera-o-Tangaroa there was no argument, for the posts were old and charred, the flax withered, and a heap of decaying inanga lay by the tuahu as an offering to the gods.

"You see?" said Ihenga.

Tu-o-Rotorua knew he had been tricked, but still hoped to disprove the claim of the interloper.

"Show me your net," he said.

Ihenga pointed to the raw scar of a landslip on a distant cliff at Te Ngae. "There is my net," he said. Tu-o-Rotorua had no reply to make, for the fresh mottled earth against the dark rocks and green bush looked like a fishing net. He bowed to the inevitable.

"What is the name of the island?" Tu-o-Rotorua asked, indicating Mokoia.

"Motutapu-a-Tinirau, the name that I gave it long ago."

"Will you consent to my people living there?"

"Yes," said Ihenga, smiling to himself at the thought of giving to another an island that did not belong to him.

And in that manner Ihenga took possession of the mainland of Rotorua.

The sharing of the name of the lake and of the chief

can hardly be accidental. An alternative form was Tua-Rotorua.

There are several claimants to the discovery and naming of the lake. Sir Peter Buck has said that Kahu-mata-momoe, the younger son of Tama-te-kapua, also visited Lake Taupo and on his return discovered Lake Rotorua and named it Te Moana-nui-a-Kahu (The big Sea of Kahu); but that the real settlers were Ika, one of the crew of *Te Arawa,* and his son, Maru-punga-nui, who lived at Okapua, where there is a pool called Te Korokoro-o-Maru-punga-nui (The Throat of Maru-punga-nui). Tua-Rotorua was the son of Maru-punga-nui.

It is Ihenga, however, whose spirit lives in the minds of lake-dwellers. There are many places round its steaming shores which are redolent of memories of the old explorer and name-giver. At Ngongotaha he settled on the bank of the Waiteti Stream to the north of Ngongotaha, and the outline of the centuries-old Weriweri kainga can still be traced. The mana of Ihenga is still powerful and his tapu lies on the land. The sacred stream Wai-oro-toki flows into the Waiteti. No Maori dared to drink there, for its waters brought death to those who did so. Close by was the Sacred Grove of Ihenga (Te Motu-tapu-a-Ihenga) and in the waters of the stream lay the tapu stone, Hine-tua-hoanga.

Three things were treasured above all else by Ihenga. There was his atua or god, Utupawa, a stone image which had come from Hawaiki, the homeland of *Te Arawa.* In the bed of the Waiteti lived the taniwha Kataore, a lizard-monster, which was afterwards killed at Tikitapu, the Blue Lake. This was the second treasure of Ihenga.

The third possession was Hine-tua-hoanga, the stone in the Wai-oro-toki River (Axe-sharpening Water). Hine-tua-hoanga is a very ancient name. In the beginning of

Hatupatu dives down to the bed of Lake Rotorua

time Tane, the god of nature, took in marriage Hine-tu-pari-maunga, the mountain girl, and Hine-tua-hoanga, the sandstone girl, was the fourth in line after that illustrious union. Here is the primeval legend. Pounamu (the personification of greenstone) quarrelled with Tutunui, the guardian of fish, who wished to keep his people in the ocean. Pounamu and Poutini, who were related to Tangaroa, the great god of the sea, disputed Tutunui's right to possession of the ocean. A battle raged between them. Tutunui called to his aid the Sandstone People, who were represented by Hine-tua-hoanga. The Sandstone People were victorious in the fight, and Hine-tua-hoanga pursued Pounamu and Poutini relentlessly to Aotearoa. Some say that the early explorer Ngahue carried the Sandstone People, but however they came, the chase went on unremittingly until at last the remnant of the Greenstone People hid themselves in a waterfall in the Arahura River, where they remained as a source of the precious stone for many generations of Maori craftsmen.

The story is highly symbolic, and is an ingenious expression of the enmity of the precious greenstone and the sandstone by which it is sharpened. According to one version, Hine-tua-hoanga was the mother of Rata, who sharpened his axe on his mother's back.

Ihenga's Hine-tua-hoanga was supposed to have been brought to New Zealand in the *Arawa* canoe. James Cowan, who was the first white man to see it, described it as a flat block of grey stone, about three feet in diameter. "In its smoothly polished surface were three deep grooves, worn by generation after generation of men in their work of 'oroorotoki', or axe-rubbing. It was light when it was brought in the canoe," said his Maori informant, "but through tapu it has become heavy through the long years of its resting in Wai-oro-toki."

Here is the ancient karakia or chant which Cowan recorded from a modern descendant of Whakaue, whose bones were buried in the sacred stream:

> There is no road,
> no way to the far south land
> save by the will of the gods,
> save by thee, O Whakarewa-in-the-sky,
> our guide to the distant places.
> Hither thou didst bring Poutini and Wharaua,
> axes made of the sacred greenstone;
> brought them o'er the ocean far.
> There, in that distant land, we'll see,
> flashing and shining in the waters,
> the sacred treasure-stone of Tangaroa,
> and the lightning-flashing stone,
> the bright and glistening stone.
> Banished be the tapu's spell,
> ere I place the sacred stone on Hine-tua-hoanga,
> the goddess of the whetstone,
> that the axe-blade may be sharp
> to fell the great totara tree.
> Oh come, ancestral shades!
> Come hither, ancient spirits,
> spirits of the distant places,
> come, sharpen me my stone axe-blade
> to hew me down the woods of Tane,
> to make fly the chips of Tu-kehu,*
> the son of Mumuwhango,
> the forest-child for whom we sought,
> to cross the flowing waters.

There is another rock which has a special significance for the Maori. It is Te Mauri-ohorere-a-Hatupatu (The

---

*Personification of the totara tree, son of Mumuwhango, who was one of the wives of the god Tane.

Taoi poises for the dive

startled Soul of Hatupatu). After his flight from the bird woman (see Chapter 13), Hatupatu dived from Sulphur Point and swam under water to Mokoia Island. When halfway there he felt hungry and paused to make a meal of the shellfish kakahu. The place of his underwater meal is known by the long white rock on the lake bed. It was held in awe, for the sight of it was considered a fatal portent and a crew unfortunate enough to see it in the shallow water was doomed to an early death.

From Owhata, the village where Hinemoa lived, a long shoal stretches across the lake to Kawaha. The Maori used to have a peculiar belief that the surface of the water above the shoal was heaped up in a ridge, and to this unnatural phenomenon he gave the name Te Hiwi-o-te-toroa (The Ridge of the Albatross).

Long ago the chief Uenuku was paddling over the ridge in his canoe, accompanied by his three wives. One of them, Taoi, was elaborately tattooed on thighs and buttocks, and Uenuku, proud of this adornment of his wife, was anxious that his other wives should see it. Perhaps he felt some embarrassment at asking her to display her charms, so he accomplished his purpose in a more subtle fashion by suggesting a diving competition. The object of the competition was to see who could bring up some of the fresh-water mussel from the sandbank underneath.

Taoi dropped her cloak, stood upright and dived far below, but while she was poised for the dive the tattooing was seen and admired by the others. Murmuring an incantation, Taoi held her breath and went lower and lower, out of sight of the watchers in the canoe. Presently an albatross feather floated to the surface. It had broken away from Taoi's ear, and a few moments later she appeared, smiling triumphantly as she held up a handful of sand to prove that she had touched the sandbank.

It was in memory of this dive and of the feather that floated to the surface that the "ridge" of water was called the ridge of the albatross.

There were hazards in the lake. The white rock of Hatupatu was one, but wary crews knew where it lay and were able to avoid it. Rongomai, a tipua or supernatural being, was more difficult to avoid. Rongomai took the form of a fern-tree which floated on the lake, with one end emerging from the water like a snag. It was an evil omen to gaze upon Rongomai, for the floating tree was possessed of magic powers which could blast a man's life. It is said that if paddlers came on it when it lay floating in the calm water or travelling as if driven on by some malign power, their lives would speedily become forfeit to the black magic of Rongomai.

Chapter Seven

MOKOIA ISLAND

"I KAPI I TE TANGATA," they used to say of the island of Mokoia — "covered with men." It is only a small island, about a mile square, protected by the encircling waters, rising in proud isolation 500 feet above the level of the lake, and with a history of more than a thousand years. It was the home of the dead as well as of the living, for it was a place of secret burial for those of high rank, and for this reason was spoken of as Mokoia the Parent. Visitors would sometimes take a handful of earth or leaves when they left to keep in cherished memory of this sacred spot.

The tapu of the island protects even the little gulls which frequent it. The spirits of the dead were supposed to enter into them, and the leaders of the flocks were believed to be the renowned and ancient chiefs of the Arawa tribe.

The island history, steeped in tradition, begins long before the coming of the *Arawa* canoe, when Raupo-Ngaoheohe (the Rustling Reeds), and Tururu-mauku (the Drooping Ferntrees) were the people of Mokoia. Then came the Arawa folk, conquering the primitive people, and Ihenga gave the name which came first from distant Hawaiki — Te Motutapu-a-Tinirau, The Sacred Isle of Tinirau. Ihenga had arrived at the point known as Tuara-hiwi-roa in his journeyings, and saw a flock of shags perched on tree stumps in the lake. Ihenga and his followers made a snare, which they placed on a pole. After a time the shags were caught in the snare, but they were so numerous that when they attempted to free themselves they lifted the snare and the pole, and flew off with it.

"They will alight on the lake," a young man said, but Ihenga disagreed.

"No, they will keep on flying," he said. "They will fly as far as Te Motutapu-a-Tinirau," and that was when the island first received its name.

Its later name, Mokoia, is a curious example of a native pun. Many years went by before the original inhabitants were finally exterminated or absorbed by the Arawa tribe. One of these aboriginals was Arorangi, chief of the Kawa-Arero tribe, who had killed and eaten a dog belonging to Uenuku-kopako. As a result a local battle was fought and Arorangi was killed by an Arawa chief. He was struck over the eye with the sharp point of a ko, or digging implement. The wound was made where his face was closely tattooed. When Uenuku heard of this he called the name of the battle Mokoia, which means tattooed, and is also a play on the words moko (tattoo) and ko (digging implement). The name of the battle was afterwards transferred to the island.

One of the many things for which the island is notable

The kumara god of Mokoia Island

is Te Matua-tonga, a kumara god, a stone emblem of fertility. It is about four feet high and was brought to Aotearoa by the *Arawa* canoe. For many years it has been kept in a tiny wooden building which may almost be described as a miniature temple. In the planting season the tribes of the district went on a pilgrimage to Mokoia, carrying seed-kumara. They touched the sacred effigy with the seed to ensure the fertility of their crop. In the warm, volcanic soil the little god protected the plantations against blight and frost.

"*Kia tu tangatanga te aro ki Mokoia*" (Let the way be open to Mokoia) was a saying which recognised the power of Te Matua-tonga. A charming song was recorded by James Cowan:

> Who will feast upon
> The stores of dried fish yonder?
> The throats of the people of Mokoia,
> The place of the well-filled ovens,
> Will be a relish for us
> To go down with the kumara.
> Aha! How sweet it will be.

Above the shrine of Te Matua-tonga is a famous totara tree, known as Te Pare-a-Hatupatu, which grew from a twig in a chaplet of leaves worn by Hatupatu. In another tapu spot is a grove of trees, containing a venerable tawa, also known as Te Pare-a-Hatupatu (The Head-wreath of Hatupatu). There must have been a singular potency in the chaplet of Hatupatu, for the pohutukawas which fringe the shores of the island are also supposed to have sprung from the same source.

In the year 1823 the islanders suffered severe losses from the Nga-Puhi of the far north, led by the redoubtable chief Hongi Hika. At this time Hongi was the most feared man in New Zealand. Three years earlier he had taken

MOKOIA ISLAND

ship to England, where King George IV granted him an audience and gave him a suit of armour and other gifts. At Sydney, on his way back to New Zealand, he exchanged many of these presents for muskets and ammunition, and on arrival at the Bay of Islands lost no time in achieving his ambition of becoming the overlord of the tribes. The pas were helpless against warriors armed with the weapons of the pakeha, and Hongi's raids became a bloody procession of victories. It was in the early part of 1823 that Hongi set out with a flotilla of canoes and an army of bloodthirsty fighting men to subdue Te Arawa.

The people of Rotorua, aware that Hongi would have to march overland to reach their settlement, considered themselves impregnable in the fortress of Mokoia, with the vast moat of the lake as their protection. But Hongi was better armed and more cunning than his opponents. His canoes were paddled up the Pongakawa River and were then hauled overland. The stretch of modern highway known as Hongi's Track recalls that memorable feat. The moat that was to have protected the Arawa people became a highway of vengeance as Hongi's canoes paddled across Rotoehu and Rotoiti and through the Ohau Channel to Rotorua.·

Early one morning, while the mists still lay heavy on the lake, Te Arawa slept peacefully. The sentries were on watch, but could see nothing through the mist. Suddenly a flock of gulls flew up in alarm from the sand bank. The Arawa people were alerted as the gulls screamed overhead and they rushed to defend the beaches. From that ill-omened morning, the watchful gulls of Mokoia have been held in reverence by the Arawa, who will allow no one, Maori or pakeha, to molest the sacred birds, in whose bodies, they say, still live the spirits of warriors who died in battle.

The warning of the gulls

MOKOIA ISLAND

Hongi was in no hurry to subdue the fortifications. For three days his canoes ominously encircled the island. Even so, some of the Arawa people escaped by swimming to the mainland at night. When Hongi's men opened fire and made their bridgehead on the northern shore, the guns mowed down the opposition, and the Nga-Puhi were soon in possession of the island. Aue! The warning of the birds was in vain, for great were the losses of Arawa. But they gave a good account of themselves.

Many of Hongi's men were killed, and the chief himself had a narrow escape when his helmet was shot from his head and he was knocked over in his canoe. If he had intended to occupy the island and the adjacent territory permanently, he changed his mind and, after making a truce with Hikairo, the Arawa chief, he returned to his home, taking many prisoners with him.

The years passed by. The Queen's peace came to New Zealand and Hori Kerei, Sir George Grey, well-loved by the Arawa, visited the island. He recorded the stories they delighted to tell him.

"Our famous ancestor, Tuhourangi, is buried here," they told him. "He was a man among men. He measured six feet up to his arm pits. He was nine feet tall!"

Perhaps the Governor eyed his informants quizzically, for he was informed that the bones were buried near the Pukurahi pa and that their story could be proved. A little more conversation and then men set to work to disinter the bones — but they could not be found. "But they are there!" say Arawa, for the sacred bones of their ancestor could not be defiled by the gaze even of Hori Kerei, and the men had deliberately dug in the wrong place. Surely tradition cannot be wrong, for it is said that in earlier days Tuhourangi's bones were set up on the edge of the kumara plantations each year to ensure the fertility of an already fertile crop.

With the legend of Hinemoa and Tutanekai, Grey was more fortunate. Did he not see Wai-kimihia, the warm pool of Hinemoa, and Kawa-te-tangi, the site of Tutanekai's home? The story is the best-known, best-loved in all Maoriland.

The young chief Tutanekai lived with his parents and brothers on the island. On the occasion of a tribal visit to the lakeside village of Owhata, Tutanekai saw and promptly fell in love with the beautiful puhi or high-born young chieftainess of Owhata. Young women of Hinemoa's status were closely guarded, and Tutanekai had had no opportunity of declaring his love when it was time to return to Mokoia.

Hinemoa had noticed the ardent glances of the young man. What the tongue had been unable to convey was spoken through the eyes in the language lovers know best.

Each night Tutanekai stood on the verandah of his whare looking over the dark waters towards Owhata, thinking of Hinemoa. After a while he brought out his nose-flute and breathed into it the melody of a love song which stole across the water and found its way to Hinemoa's heart.

The days and nights dragged slowly, until at last another visit was made to Owhata by the tribe of Mokoia. There was no need for any protestation of love. While the dancers of Owhata entertained their guests the lovers stood outside in the shadow.

"How shall we meet?" Tutanekai asked.

"I will come to you, Tutanekai, my beloved. But I must come alone without telling anyone. How shall I know when you will be ready?"

"I am always ready. But we must take care for I could

not bear to be parted from you. Tomorrow night I will play the flute. When you hear the music, come quietly down to the beach and take a small canoe. Paddle across the lake and I will be waiting for you."

The next night the music of the flute came soft and clear across the water. When everyone was asleep, Hinemoa crept down to the beach, but to her consternation she found that the canoes had all been pulled well up the sand and into the bush. She did not have sufficient strength to drag even the smallest canoe across the boulders. The flute played on unheeded as she returned sadly to the sleeping house.

The next night she hurried down in the darkness, but the canoes were still out of reach. Then she knew that her plans had been suspected, for some of the craft had been in use during the day, and would not normally have been pulled up into the bush.

Night after night went by and her heart seemed to call out in desperation as the flute song pulsed in the still night air, seeking for Hinemoa who could not come.

Secretly she prepared six empty gourds, tying them with flax. On the first moonlight night she went down to the beach, cast off her cloak, and tied the gourds firmly round her body.

As the flute song came faintly with the wind, died away and swelled again, she slipped into the cold water and began swimming with strong, slow strokes toward the island. The breeze was making tiny waves which hit her face sharply and drowned the sound of the flute. Everything was dark and the girl felt panic rising lest she should miss her way. She stopped and listened, but there was no sound except the lapping of the waters. She swam on again and felt a sharp pain in her arm. Something blacker than the surrounding darkness towered over her. She gave a cry, thinking that perhaps it was a taniwha of the deep lake.

But it was only a log floating in the water. Hinemoa grasped it and lifted herself partly out of the water and as she did so the notes of the flute came clearly on the breeze. With a sigh of thankfulness she swam on again.

When next she listened the music had gone, for it was late and Tutanekai had given up hope. The girl swam on with strength and courage failing but her heart quickened as she heard the hiss of water on a sandy beach. Her knee struck the sand and, overcome with relief, she staggered up the beach, half dead with cold.

Hinemoa felt her way carefully until she touched rocks which were strangely warm. There was a smell of sulphur-laden steam and a few moments later she lowered her body cautiously into the luxurious warmth of a hot pool. She knew then where she was, for this was the pool Wai-kimihia, which lay directly below Tutanekai's whare.

As her body gratefully received the warmth, she began to think. The spirit of adventure and the call of her heart had sustained her, but now she felt ashamed of her nakedness. She heard footsteps on the path leading down from her lover's whare and hid behind the boulders for the first paling of the sky in the east had lightened the darkness.

As Hinemoa peered over the rocks she made out the form of a man lowering something into the water. Disguising her voice she spoke like a man: "Who are you?"

The unknown man started. "I am filling a calabash for my master."

"Who is your master?"

"Tutanekai."

Hinemoa's heart leaped in her breast. "Give me the calabash."

The frightened slave passed it over and she drank from it. Then she hurled it against the rocks, where it broke into a dozen pieces.

The slave gave a cry of alarm. "You will pay for this. Who are you?"

Hinemoa had sunk out of sight behind the rocks, and there was no answer. The slave stood up and ran back to the whare.

"Where is the water?" Tutanekai asked. "I am thirsty and cannot sleep."

"I haven't got it," the slave replied in a trembling voice. "When I got to the pool a man took the calabash from me and broke it."

Tutanekai was too wretched to care. He had been tossing restlessly on his sleeping mat, wondering whether Hinemoa had forsaken him.

"Take another calabash," he said crossly, "and don't drop it this time."

The slave went down more cautiously. He looked round, but no one was there. He stooped, but as the water lipped the rim of the vessel, the same deep voice he had heard before said, "That is Tutanekai's calabash. Give it to me."

A hand came round the rocks and plucked the calabash from the slave's nerveless fingers. Again there was a crash as the water-vessel struck the rocks; again there was a panic-stricken rush up the path.

Tutanekai raised himself on his elbow.

"This is my last time of telling," he said. "You have been careless, but if it happens again you will regret it. Now bring me the water."

Reluctantly the slave went down to the pool. It was growing light but he still feared the unknown. At the first sound of the deep voice he fled back to his master's

Tutanekai finds his lover

whare. The sound of a shattering calabash echoed behind him.

"It is not my fault," he told Tutanekai breathlessly. "I tell you there is a man there. You know I would not break your calabash three times. He asked if it was yours, and then he broke it."

At last Tutanekai was roused. He tied his maro round his waist, caught up a mere and ran down to the pool. Hinemoa heard him coming. It was not the slave, for these footfalls were light and swift.

Tutanekai stood by the brink of the pool, his eyes straining to pierce the half-light.

"Where are you, breaker of pots?" he demanded quietly. "Come out like a man, not like a koura that lurks in the crannies of the rocks."

There was no reply, for Hinemoa had sunk down so deep that her hair floated like seaweed on the still water. Tutanekai circled the pool until his eyes became accustomed to the darkness. Then he put down his hand and grasped the hair.

"There you are, pot-breaker," he said grimly. "Let me see your face. Who are you?"

Slowly Hinemoa stood upright in the light of early morning, facing her lover with an uncertain smile.

"I am Hinemoa."

The dawn stood still and the waves were silent in that moment of union as the lovers melted in their first embrace.

* * * *

The morning meal was eaten and still there was no sign of Tutanekai. The door of his whare was shut.

"Where is your master?" they asked the slave.

"I do not know. I have not seen him since he went to the pool to see the stranger who broke his calabashes. Perhaps he is sleeping now, because he was disturbed in the night."

Tutanekai's father leaped to his feet. "And perhaps he is down by the pool," he said scornfully. "Who is the stranger who breaks calabashes at night? It may be that my son has been killed! Open the door."

The slave hurried to the whare and pulled the sliding door. He peered inside.

"There are four feet here," he cried. "Someone is with Tutanekai."

Every eye was fixed on the door as Tutanekai came proudly out into the sunlight holding his bride's hand.

The old man hurried towards them. "It is Hinemoa!" he said, holding out his hand, and the people echoed his cry: "Hinemoa! Welcome to Hinemoa!"

But Tutanekai's brothers were jealous. "It cannot be Hinemoa," they murmured. "There is no canoe on the beach, and women are not birds to fly across the water."

Then Tutanekai told the story of her swim across the dark waters, and they knew it was true, for they had heard his flute in the night. And indeed Hinemoa stood before them herself in all her proud beauty to show that love is greater than many waters.

* * * *

You, pakeha, who visit Mokoia, may still see Kawa-te-tangi, the site of Tutanekai's home, and the stone-rimmed pool where Hinemoa hid herself in the warm waters of Wai-kimihia so many years ago. And you will remember this simple story which will always be told by the people of Maoriland.

CHAPTER EIGHT

LAKE-SIDE VILLAGES AND SPRINGS

AS WE TRAVEL ROUND THE LAKE from Rotorua, we come first to the tiny settlement of Owhata, the home of Hinemoa, on the eastern shore. One of the carved houses bears her name, and near it is the rock Iriiri-kapua where she sat and listened to Tutanekai's flute.

Te Ngae

A mile or two north of Owhata is Te Ngae (The Swamp). Long ago this place was the home of a noted warrior named Rangi-te-ao-rere (Flying Cloud), and his descendants have lived there ever since. His story is an interesting one. Rangi was the illegitimate son of a warrior who lived at Tikitere and a chieftainess of the Urewera. When Rangi reached manhood he felt an overpowering desire to find his father. Taking with him a band of 140 fighting men and many gifts from his mother, Rangi crossed the endless ranges until he neared Lake Rotoiti. The taua passed the dangerous taniwha Kataore, who lived on the Matawhaura Range, in safety. This taniwha lay beside the track, its open jaws propped up by a great rock. If passers-by gave it food, it was content with their offering, but if they tried to pass without making an offering, the taniwha promptly ate the travellers. Rangi was forewarned. He presented the taniwha with a large basket of food, and while Kataore was occupied with it, the taua passed by.

Rangi kept a sharp look-out, for his mother had said, "When you see the steam of hot springs, you will know that you are on the right road to your father."

Presently they came to Tikitere and Rangi knew that the large whare on the hill must belong to his father. The party was welcomed by the occupants of the pa. On Rangi's orders they took up a position in front of the chief's whare, while he went round to the back. To the amazement of the onlookers he climbed through the tapu window and sat on his father's bed. To make matters worse, Rangi called to his followers to bring food into the house.

This was sacrilege! Messengers were sent post-haste to Rangi-whakaeke-hau, Rangi's father. "A party of travellers has entered your house," they gasped. "They have taken food into it. One of them has even seated himself on your sleeping place, and used your red ochre!"

Rangi the elder ran to his house and ordered the intruders to come out, but Rangi the younger stayed where he was, and sang part of a lullaby his mother used to sing to him when he was a baby. The old song stirred forgotten chords in the older man's memory.

"Are you Rangi-te-ao-rere?" he asked.

"You yourself said to my mother before I was born, 'If your child be a male, then let it be named after the drifting clouds,'" was the reply.

Then Rangi-whakaeke-hau knew that it was his son. He embraced him and his people set about preparing a feast.

Now it happened that at that time the island of Mokoia had been occupied by another tribe, and the Arawa people were anxious to capture it, but had so far been unsuccessful.

"Let your quarrel pass into my hands," Flying Cloud said boldly.

His father smiled. "How will you take possession of the island?" he asked.

"I will fight from canoes."

"That will be useless. We have already tried, but they wade out in the shallow water, take hold of the canoes and drag them ashore."

"I will do better than that," Flying Cloud said. He took the largest canoe the Arawa had, and boarded it with his 140 fighting men. They took their weapons, two long ropes and two large, sharpened stakes.

The big canoe took the lake waters like a flag ship, followed by the smaller canoes of the Arawa. When Rangi's canoe was close to the island one of the sharpened stakes was driven into the sand. The canoe backed out until the rope by which it was attached to the stake was taut. Then the other stake was driven in at the stern of the canoe and a rope attached to it. By this time the islanders had taken hold of the bow rope and endeavoured to haul the canoe ashore, but they were unable to do so, because it was attached to the stern post.

More and more of the defenders arrived and tugged at the rope. Rangi gave a signal, the stern rope was cut and the canoe jerked forward, impelled by the paddlers as well as those who were pulling on the rope. The huge waka taua (war canoe) surged onwards, tumbling the islanders in every direction, and dug its prow into the beach. Most of Rangi's men leaped ashore and engaged the enemy in combat. Others turned round and attacked the men who were in the water. These unfortunate wretches were caught between the canoe of Rangi the son, and the Arawas under Rangi the father, and were soon exterminated.

Isolated on the island, the remaining warriors were outnumbered and beaten. That night the cooking fires were kept busy, and Te Arawa were once more in possession of Mokoia.

The Flying Cloud lived there for a while. Some time later he went to Tauranga, where he had further adventures and barely escaped with his life. When he returned to Rotorua he found that his relatives had divided the island among themselves, leaving him only a rocky cliff which was unable to support his people.

It was then that he crossed over to Te Ngae, where he settled and left this village to his descendants.

One would think that after the famous exploit at Rotorua everyone would know the "rope trick", but a later version of it proved just as effective against Hongi and his Nga-Puhi warriors. A method adopted for catching the koura or small fresh-water crayfish in Lake Rotorua was to drive a post with a strong rope attached firmly into the sand at the bottom of the lake. A canoe was attached to the rope, the net paid out, and the canoe brought back by pulling on the rope.

Sometimes two canoes were used. One was tied to the post by bow and stern, and the hauling rope of the second canoe paid out from the stationary one.

After the capture of Mokoia by Hongi, the Nga-Puhi

Flying Cloud's canoe overwhelms the defenders of Mokoia Island

were anxious to sample these luxuries. They took a party of their prisoners to a famous fishing ground just off the shore at Te Ngae. As the Nga-Puhi knew little of the art, their canoe was tied to the post while the Arawa experts took the smaller canoe to pay out the net.

The prisoners paddled off with the dredge-net, paying out the rope as they went. But when they came to the end of the rope, they cast it off and paddled with all their might to the shore and made their escape. The Nga-Puhi were helpless. By the time they had released their canoe from the post, the Arawas were far beyond their reach.

Mourea

On the southern shore of the Ohau Channel, which connects Rotorua and Rotoiti, once stood the pa of Mourea. Its palisaded defences were slight, for the pa was nearly surrounded by water. The name Mourea or Morea, which is said to mean Remnant, was a name imported from the Society Group by an earlier generation of Maoris.

Many tauas have passed that way. Even in comparatively modern times the peaceful neighbourhood has been disturbed by warlike preparations. In 1864, the loyal Arawas made preparations to prevent the Bay of Plenty and East Coast tribes from joining forces with the Maori King in the Waikato. Lead musket balls were feverishly prepared at Mourea from sporting ammunition supplied by the officers of the Imperial Forces at Tauranga, and from the lead lining of tea chests. The Ngati-Whakaue forces at Ohinemutu were strengthened by recruits from Tauranga. They crossed over the lake to Mourea, where the canoes were taken through the channel, and launched an attack on the Kingite Maoris on Rotoiti.

The channel was named by Ihenga when he first came to Lake Rotorua. His dog, Hau, was swimming across the

Hamurana Springs, the home of Hinerua

river and was drowned in a whirlpool, and from that incident, Ihenga called the channel Ohau (The place of Hau).

HAMURANA SPRINGS

The crystal-clear waters of Hamurana have had three names — Kaikai-tahuna, the more widely-known Te Puna-i-Hangarua (The Spring of Hangarua), and its present name. Strange as it may seem, the modern name Hamurana is of missionary origin. Hamurana is the Maori pronunciation of Smyrna, the famous Greek city founded by Alexander the Great in Asia Minor, and referred to in the Book of Revelation as one of the Seven Churches. In its Maori form it is as beautiful and melodious as the smooth-flowing waters of the stream.

The deep, tree-sheltered spring which wells up so

strongly that pennies dance in its waters has a flow of a million gallons an hour. Here, in its mysterious depth, a gentle taniwha was once reputed to have made its home. The taniwha of the hot lakes were well known for their voracity, but Hinerua, the taniwha of Te Puna-i-Hangarua, was a remarkable exception. It was a female of the species and was regarded as the pet of a nearby chieftainess. Hinerua sometimes left the cold depths of her spring and paid a visit to her mistress, walking delicately round the kumara plantations and peering through the gaps in the palisades, but she did no harm to the tribespeople.

When the chieftainess died, Hinerua was never seen again. Perhaps she went to keep her mistress company in the twilight underworld. The little blind fish that live deep in the waters of the spring are known as the children of Hinerua.

Taniwha Springs

Three miles from Hamurana there are sixteen small springs of waters, known collectively as Taniwha Springs. It is a pleasant spot, in a bush-clad valley, where the green water-weed contrasts with the pink willow roots.

Although no taniwha lurk now in these crystal waters, there was a modern marvel which will some day no doubt turn from reality to legend. Amongst the swarming trout of the little stream was Harvey, a rainbow trout with a colour scheme which evoked such adjectives as "two-toned" and "Technicolored". On ordinary occasions Harvey had a distinctive colour scheme, dark-green or dark reddish-brown in front and yellow-green on the rear half of his body. At feeding time the line of demarcation disappeared and he turned light green all over. The colours continued to change until the fish was light in the front and dark at the rear. After about five minutes he would revert to his normal colour scheme. This remarkable fish had both male and female organs. The almost unbelievable Harvey died in 1956.

Te Awahou (The New River) is another of the names bestowed by the indefatigable explorer Ihenga. The river springs from a great pool, which bore the forbidding name of Te Waro-uri (The Dark Chasm). The Maori settlement took its name from the river. Taniwha Springs is a modern name which recalls a spine-chilling event which took place long ago in the Dark Chasm.

The Rotorua country was noted not only for its taniwha, of which there were four — Hotupuku, Pekehaua, Kataore and Kaiwhare — but also for the men who overcame them. There was a band of warriors, 140 in number, whose exploits are known throughout the Arawa country.

Travellers between Rotorua and the Waikato disappeared mysteriously. The place of their disappearance was narrowed down until it was discovered that Pekehaua, water-monster of the Dark Chasm, was responsible. When the news was known, the courageous party of dragon-slayers set out and camped by the Awahou stream.

They observed the habits of the monster. Realising that it was not likely to leave its water-hole while it was surrounded by armed men, they decided that the only method of overcoming it was to attack it in its lair. While some of them kept watch, others went into the forest and collected supplejack and strong creepers. With this material they made a strong trap, strengthened with twisted vines and decorated with pigeon feathers. The trap was weighted with heavy stones attached to the cage by ropes, so that it would sink in the water; an anchor was also provided to keep the cage steady.

It would have been simple to have lowered the cage to the bottom of the chasm, but that in itself was not sufficient to capture the taniwha. It needed strong and fearless men to entice the monster into the cage. The chief Pikata was chosen as the leader. Several of his companions accompanied him, and together they seized the trap and plunged into the turbulent water.

It was icy cold and the dark flood of water roared in their ears, while the taniwha lurked unseen somewhere beside them. In the dim light, roots of trees and misshapen rocks looked like monsters, but Pikata and his men clung to the sides of the cage unfearing, as it settled to the bottom of the pool.

Above them the tohungas chanted incantations to reduce the power of the taniwha. That spell of long ago, passed on from generation to generation, was recorded by Cowan:

> The monster there!
> Vast as a rock he lies!
> How angrily his eyeballs glare!
> How flash his fiery eyes;
> Come sleep, come sleep;
> Let the slumbrous spell be laid
> In depths below, in depths below.
> Let the sleep be as of night,
> Like the great night,
> The Long Night,
> The Sleep-bringing Night,
> Sleep on — sleep on!

Surely even Pikata's heart must have failed when he saw the lean flanks of Pekehaua, the glaring eyes, the saw-edged spines, and the long, curved talons of the evil monster of the darkness. The taniwha crept slowly forward, its saucer-like eyes fixed on the men in a baleful glare which lit up the inky water.

But the monster moved sluggishly; its spines were soft, for the karakia had taken effect. Leaving the cage, Pikata

The capture of the taniwha of the Dark Chasm

crept forward, closer and closer to the taniwha. If he had been on the ground he would have sprung towards it, but he was numb with cold, and he had to fight against the pressure of the surging water. His feet were swept aside and his body brushed against the dragon's jaws, which opened sluggishly.

Thrusting himself still further forward, Pikata bound the huge form with a rope. His men pulled firmly and Pekehaua was drawn into the open mouth of the cage. A sharp pull on a rope was the signal to the warriors above to draw the cage to the surface. The taniwha was so large and heavy that they would not have succeeded if the tohungas had not sung other chants which made heavy objects lighter.

Slowly the cage rose through the dark water until it came to view with Pikata and his men hanging to its sides, gasping for breath. The huge monster seemed to fill the pool. The cage shook and bent as though it were made with stalks of grass instead of tough supplejack vines. The warriors on the bank dug their heels into the ground and pulled until their sinews cracked. The cage caught on the edge of the bank and turned over. Dropping the rope, the warriors all rushed forward and beat the taniwha with clubs until its struggles ceased.

The news spread like fire in the fern, and even the most timid came to see the dreaded taniwha which now lay on the land like a stranded whale. Many were the exclamations of satisfaction, but there was fear too. A twitch of the mighty tail was enough to send many running for shelter.

There was no mistake. Pekehaua was dead and never again would lonely travellers by the Awahou disappear from sight.

The cutting knives were brought to the bank of the

The pool where the gods once played

stream, and the huge body of the taniwha was cut open.

"*Koteriu o Tane-Mahuta*" (The hollow Stomach of the Forest-god), went up the awe-stricken cry. And indeed the confusion was like the undergrowth of the dense forest, where fallen trees lie prone in every direction under the canopy of leaves.

Ah, but it was not like the clean forest. It was more like a cave covered with bones, the bones of those who had been devoured by the taniwha. And not only bones! Many of the victims had been swallowed whole. There were precious possessions of those who had lost their lives in the Dark Chasm — clubs, taiahas, spears — until it looked like a store-house of weapons.

The Arawa people wept over these sacred relics of their friends and took their revenge on the dead body of Pekehaua. They cut off the flesh and roasted it, and what was left over after they had satisfied themselves was preserved in fat, and the camping place they called Mangungu (Broken Bones).

Fairy Springs

To the south of Ngongotaha, we come to the well known as Fairy Springs — the Puna-a-Tuhoe of the Maori.

To the old time Maori, legends clustered as thickly round this delightful fairy-land pool as the rainbow trout which weave a living pattern of colour in the clear waters. The name itself was famous, for Puna-a-Tuhoe means the Spring of Tuhoe, who was the ancestor of the Tuhoe tribe (People of the Mist) in the Urewera ranges.

Tuhoe lived in his strongly-fortified pa, Karaka, on the summit of the hill that overlooks the springs. He could see the gleam of water amongst the trees that shaded its cool depths, and called this his Wai-whakaruku-hanga-atua (Pool where the Gods Plunge).

Brightly though the waters sparkle in the sunshine now, cheerful as the laughter of children running along the paths over the little rustic bridges, carefree though the tourists may be, the ancient tapu once lay heavy on the Fairy Springs.

Tuhoe's priests were powerful. They were the mediums of the war gods, and when meteors blazed across the sky, it was a signal to the impatient warriors. The flaming stars showed the path to victory, and no toa would hesitate to follow its fiery trail. As the taua left on its deadly errand, Tu-nui-te-ika and Te Pou-tuatini, the gods of war, returned to their home and plunged into the living water of the Fairy Springs — the pool where the gods once played.

Its modern name seems a pale, fabricated pakeha name, but it may serve to remind us of the fairies who used to descend the slope of misty Ngongotaha to drink its water.

Chapter Nine

NGONGOTAHA

NGONGOTAHA IS A MALE MOUNTAIN. His wife is gentle Moerangi, to the south of the lake on the way to Tarawera. When Moerangi puts on her cap of cloud, it is a sign that she is asking her husband whether he will permit rain to come to the lake district. If Ngongotaha dons his cloud cap, the weather will turn to rain, but so long as his head is clear, the rain will hold off, no matter how Moerangi longs for it.

From this it will be seen that Ngongotaha is a mountain of great mana. It is notable, amongst all the mountains of Maoriland, as the home of the fairy people, and on its summit is Te Tuaha-o-te-atua, the very altar of the god.

It is believed that the mountain was the home of the tangata-whenua, the people of the land who preceded the Maoris of the Great Migration by hundreds of years. It is amongst the nearly forgotten tribes of the shadowy past that we may find the progenitors of the fairies, pale

Ihenga throws his torch into the bracken

ghosts of later years, who have flitted through the bush of Ngongotaha.

Fairies — but not the delicate, ethereal sprites of English folklore. They are white, robust, tall and terrifying — a natural evolution from the aboriginal people. The Maoris called them patu-paiarehe, turehu and other names, and the English word "fairies" is too genteel and dainty a word for the strange denizens of the forests.

It was Ihenga the explorer who first discovered the patu-paiarehe of Ngongotaha as he peered into every nook and cranny of the environs of Lake Rotorua. Though the mist swathed the mountains, he was not daunted by the plaintive songs that rose and fell in the dripping forest. He pressed on boldly up the slopes of the mountain. All about him he heard doleful piping and from the corner of his eye he saw strange forms and movements which showed that his progress was being followed.

A shift of wind cleared the mist from the peak. Ihenga stopped and saw the palisades of the fairy pa and, closer at hand, a tree which blazed like a torch. Perhaps it had been struck by a random flash of lightning. He approached it and grasped a branch from which the flame blossomed.

There was a patter of feet behind him and a shout, "A nanakia!" Ihenga stepped back as the patu-paiarehe rushed him. He swung the flaming branch round him and plunged it quickly into the bracken. The dry stems flared up. The flames raced up the slopes towards the pa and the fairy men took refuge in the dense bush, while Ihenga fled down the hillside.

Later Ihenga became friendly with the mysterious people of the bush, and this nearly led to his undoing. On one occasion he visited the pa on the mountain top and, feeling thirsty, accepted a drink from the calabash of a fairy woman. It may have been too generous a sense of hospitality which prompted the gift — perhaps a desire to keep the chief with them for all time. There was enchantment in the water. When he had drunk it, great fear fell on Ihenga, and he fled from the fairy people in panic, crashing through the undergrowth, with the patu-paiarehe in full chase after him.

Closest of all came the woman who had given him the water, her hands stretched out to seize him as she ran. Without slackening his pace, Ihenga fumbled in the folded pocket of his girdle. His fingers touched the sacred red ochre and shark-oil he kept in the pocket. He smeared it hastily over his naked body. The result was seen immediately. The smell nauseated the fairy woman, who fell back. Her companions were equally fearful and disgusted with the smell of oil and the sight of the red ochre, which was so repugnant to them, and Ihenga made his escape.

It was this incident which is supposed to have given the name to the mountain,* for ngongo is the funnel or mouth-piece of a taha, or calabash. To the fanciful, the mountain may also be likened to a gourd or calabash lying on its side. And so the mountain, the stream and later the railway station and pakeha village gained this unusual name.

It is said that Ihenga stole the kauae, the jaw bone of a moa, from the patu-paiarehe pa, and therefore bestowed the name Te Kauae upon the steep precipice on the flank of Ngongotaha, which leans towards the lake. There the lightning sometimes flashes three times in quick succession. Then the Arawa people know that a chief will die, for this is their rua-koha, the flashing of a hand that opens and shuts to say that death will come to a rangatira. There

---

*Another legend has it that the chief Te Rangipere lived near the summit of Ngongotaha, and that it was he who made a drinking tube for his calabash in order to preserve his tapu.

Ihenga flees from the fairy people of Ngongotaha

must have been an uneasy truce between Ihenga and the patu-paiarehe in the years that followed, for the Ngati-Whatua often heard the thin piping voices of the fairies, and learned their songs, when they lived in the pa Whakaeka-tahina by the Waiteti Stream.

As the Maori tribes grew in number the fairies were forced further and further away. Fires destroyed the dense bush, until at length the patu-paiarehe chief Tongakohu led his people away from the haunts of the Maori. Some of them went to Moehau (Cape Colville) and others went to Mount Pirongia in the Waikato. Both these mountains were noted for their grim fairy population. Some of them may even yet cling to Ngongotaha, in spite of the tourist buses which drive right up to the site of their dreaded pa. Not long ago, Joyce West wrote of the mountain:

"But when the mists lie upon the breast of the waters, and the swirling storm clouds reach down to enwrap the brooding summit of Ngongotaha, then . . . the Maoris say . . . you may hear the thin sweet music of the fairy flutes, the putorino, drifting down from the mountainside. Then, it may be, that the fairies are abroad, and Unuaho the Wizard walks his ways again, then you may hear . . . if you listen at the hour of nightfall . . . the singing tree of Tona whispering across the misty water."

As we say farewell to Ngongotaha, let us read the "Lochaber no more" of the departing Tongakohu, a lament that was preserved by the Arawa people for many generations, and translated by James Cowan.

    Night's shadows fall,
    Sharp sorrow eats my heart,
    Grief for the home I'm leaving,
    For my sacred sleeping-place.
    The home-pillow I'm leaving,
    On Ngongo's lofty peak.
    So lone my mountain stands,
    Swept by the flames of Mahuika.*
    I'm going far away,
    To the heights of Moehau, to Pirongia,
    To seek another home.
    O Rotokohu! Leave me yet awhile;
    Let me farewell my forest shrine,
    The Tuahu I'm leaving.
    Give me but one more day:
    Just one more day, and then I'll go,
    And I'll return no more.

*The goddess of fire, grandmother of Maui.

CHAPTER TEN

TIKITERE

WHEN GEORGE BERNARD SHAW visited Tikitere during his Dominion tour he said that he was pleased to have the opportunity to get so close to Hades and yet be able to return, a privilege which he had never expected during his long and chequered life.

With a background of Biblical imagery and classic myth, the pakeha has let his imagination run riot at the "Inferno" of the thermal regions. The Devil's Cauldron, Hell's Gate, The Inferno, The Devil's Porridge Pot, Satan's Glory, Satan's Boiling Kettle of Dough and Mixing Trough, Satan's Claret Cup, the Tar and Pitch Pot — they are all manifestations of the horrifying mythological parallels which occur to the white man and, somewhat paradoxically, an evidence of infertility of imagination. "In its Dantesque horror and sublime desolation it is unapproachable," said an old guide book. "It is not that the whole valley is blasted and abominable. . . . And beauty of the surroundings only emphasises the stygian blackness of the

The greatly loved daughter of Tikitere

wife. She felt that his conduct was an insult, and in true fierce boiling waters that surge and whirl in countless cauldrons over the bottom of the valley."

The Maori knew nothing of Pluto, nor of Hades and the Inferno, but through this desolate valley of repugnant geysers, cauldrons and solfataras he wove a thread of legend no less terrifying than the white man's infernal fancies.

Tikitere was occupied by the Ngati-Rangi-te-ao-rere hapu (sub-tribe) of Arawa. Rangi-te-ao-rere was the famous Flying Cloud whose story has been told in the section on Te Ngae, the little settlement close to Tikitere which later became a mission station.

As a reward for his service, Flying Cloud was presented in marriage with a beautiful young woman of high rank named Huritini. For a while they lived happily together, but after a time Rangi-te-ao-rere neglected his young

Maori fashion she determined to wipe out the stain of degradation with her life. One night she ended her misery by plunging into the mud cauldron which still bears her name.*

When the sad news was made known to her people, they cried in anguish, "*Taku tiki i tere*" (Our greatly loved daughter has floated away). Tiki is an affectionate diminutive of potiki (child, or youngest child), and tere means floated. So it is that Hell's Gate to the Maori is Tikitere, the dear child who was carried away in the boiling pool.

An earlier legend tells us of the origin of this place of strange thermal phenomena. Between Tikitere and Lake Okataina lies the Whakapoungakau Range — a pleasant name, composed of whakapou (to establish firmly) and ngakau (heart). In the far-off days when Ngatoro-i-rangi ranged through the thermal regions, there were no boiling springs in the valley of Tikitere. It was a peaceful spot which was visited by Tane-whakaraka and his sisters, Kuiwai and Haungaroa, who had come from Hawaiki.

After their long travels they rested in the sheltered, sunlit valley. The forests on the surrounding hills rang with the song of birds. While the sisters prepared a comfortable camp site, Tane made long, slender bird spears, and troughs set with snares for the beautiful kereru (pigeons). When his preparations were complete he went into the ranges on a bird-hunting expedition. Night fell and the lonely camp-fire sent its beacon light into the darkness, but Tane did not return. Day after day his sisters waited for him, but in vain.

At length they realised that he would never return, and they departed for their home in Hawaiki. The range of

*The name is appropriate to the pool. It means ever-circling.

The lake of the shags

mountains where their brother was lost they called the Hills of Longing, the place where they had fixed their hearts; and in the little valley they left a love-token. They prayed to Ruaimoko, god of volcanic fire, who heated the pools and the tumbling cascades, so that if Tane-whakaraka ever returned to the valley, he would be able to bathe his tired body in the refreshing water.

The spirit of Tane-whakaraka might well prefer the tiny Lake Rotokawau, about a mile from Tikitere. This clear, cold lake nestling in the crater of an extinct volcano has been described by Joyce West as least and loveliest in the thermal country; and by Cowan as "a blue eye of a lake, shut in between green hills and wooded cliffs, a place of seeming mystery and enchantment".

Now lonely and isolated, the lake once had a native village beside the shore, and canoes crossed the still water.

The lake was noted for its fish, fresh-water crayfish, whitebait and shellfish, which were a constant attraction to kawau, the shag. These expert fishers gave their name to the tiny lake.

Chapter Eleven

ROTOITI AND HONGI'S TRACK

IT IS DIFFICULT to pass judgment on the varied lakes of the thermal country, for there are many preferences, and each has its own charms. With cliffs and bays thick with pohutukawas, Rotoiti offers beauty to those who love to explore its waters by launch. Many years ago it was frequented by canoes, which crossed and recrossed from the villages which crowded the beaches of silver sand.

For centuries its shores have been peopled, in decreasing numbers as the years march on, by the Ngati-Pikiao. To them came a moment of pride when, in the midst of their strenuous tour in December 1953 and January 1954, Queen Elizabeth II and the Duke of Edinburgh spent a few days in seclusion at Moose Lodge, near Tapuaekura village and the church where the first Christian mission to the people of Pikiao was established. The first visit of their well-loved Sovereign and her distinguished husband was a moment of ecstasy in the long history of Arawa and an opportunity to recall their pride of race: "May it please your Majesty, on behalf of yourself and your esteemed husband that the Ngati-Pikiao tribe, forever unswerving in their loyalty to the Crown, greets you and affirms the solemn pledge of loyalty given to Queen Victoria during the risings of the 'Kingite' movement of 1864 to 1870; a pledge given by the Arawa Confederation of Tribes, of which the Ngati-Pikiao is a member, and re-affirming to each and every one of your predecessors of the family of Queen Victoria; a pledge tested in the years of battle of the risings of the 'Kingites' and in the Maori-Pakeha skirmishes of 1864-70; in the Boer War; the First and Second World Wars and the Korean War."*

The name Rotoiti (Little Lake) is misleading, for it is nine miles in length and from two to three miles wide. To the explorer Ihenga, however, the description seemed appropriate, for at the time of its discovery he saw only the small extent of the lake at its western end. He claimed it for his children, and named it Te Roto-iti-kite-a-Ihenga (The Little Lake seen by Ihenga). The story of its discovery has already been told on page 17.

It was at Te Ruaki-o-te-kuri-a-Ihenga (The Vomit of Ihenga's Dog) that Ihenga's dog gorged itself on the whitebait which teemed in the shallows. On a nearby cliff above the lovely bay of Ohoukaka grows a weathered old pohutukawa tree which is famous in legend. Tapuae, the pohutukawa, is a wind omen, a singing tree which acted like a barometer and weather report to the inhabitants of the pa. When the branches murmured drowsily like a blowfly, it was a sign that there would be fair weather and blue skies, and it was safe to launch canoes. If the tree

*The Book of Ngati-Pikiao, an album presented to Her Majesty Queen Elizabeth II and to His Royal Highness the Duke of Edinburgh, January 1954.

whistled it was an indication of coming wind and rain. But if the whistle rose to a shrill screaming, then storms would sweep across the lake, and the canoes were pulled out of the reach of the waves. These weather forecasts were made well in advance, according to modern practice.

A tale is told of Kakanui, the ancient village of the singing tree. It was occupied by the Tuhourangi tribe whose descendants now live at Whakarewarewa. One of the young warriors of Kakanui was married to a high-born young woman who was sister of the chief Te Rangi-wawahia of Ngati-Pikiao.

Te Rangi occasionally visited Kakanui in spite of the fact that Ngati-Pikiao were almost constantly at war with Tuhourangi. The customs of the Maori people, especially in matters of warfare, are an unending puzzle to white people. They are a blend of chivalry, cruelty, ruthlessness, deceit and quixotic kindnesses. The fact that Te Rangi was related to a woman in the pa enabled him to pay a courtesy visit within the stronghold of his enemies.

During one of his visits he heard that his sister had been insulted in some way. He determined to avenge the wounded honour of his family but, knowing from his visits how strongly the cliff-top pa was guarded, he resorted to guile. He visited the pa openly and spent the night in his sister's whare. During the hours of darkness his men paddled quietly down the lake and landed a selected group of commandos on the narrow beach immediately below the cliff of Kakanui. The canoes pushed off and took up a position at a little distance out on the lake. At the first flush of dawn the Ngati-Pikiao warriors chanted their war songs and shouted defiance to the sentinels of Tuhourangi. The pa was soon roused. Seeing that their enemy made no attempt to land and storm the pa, the battle-eager warriors of Kakanui rushed down to the beach of

The assault on Kakanui

Ohoukaka, launched their canoes, and were soon attacking the enemy canoes.

The sky was flushing to a brighter glow but the shadows still lay deep under the singing tree as Te Rangi slipped like another shadow to the edge of the cliff and lowered a flax rope to the toas hidden below. He raised his head and listened. Across the water came the ringing blows of taiaha on taiaha, the shouting of men, and the duller thud of greenstone biting into flesh and bone. His voice rang out full and strong like a sentinel's:

Tika tonu mai,
Tika tonu mai,
Kia ahau, e noho nei!
I-a ha, ha!

(Come straight this way,
Straight towards me,
To the spot where now I stand,
Ha, ha!)

And straight they came to him, up the dangling flax rope, while others in canoes chased the Tuhourangi to their canoe-resting-place in Ohoukaka Bay.

It was a grim day for Tuhourangi, caught between the two raging fires of Ngati-Pikiao. One after another they fell before the onslaught of their foes, and the insult offered to a high-born woman of Ngati-Pikiao was wiped out in blood.

At the eastern end of the lake is the 1,800 foot mountain Matawhaura, and beneath it the curving sandy beach Tapuae-haruru and the Motutawa peninsula. This was once the scene of a tragedy which was not uncommon in Maori history.

Many years ago there was a kainga of the Ngati-Pikiao tribe on the crest of the peninsula, overlooking the placid

The bones of Tutea are taken to the cave below the falls

waters of the lake. Amongst the inhabitants of the village was the beautiful young chieftainess Tikawe, who lived there happily with her husband. For some reason he paid a visit to Hawke's Bay and there he fell in love with a young woman of Ngati-Kahungunu.

Daily Tikawe stood on the edge of the cliff watching for the first appearance of her husband, but in vain. The moons waxed and waned and gradually hope turned to despair.

At length she knew that he would never return. Decking herself in her best cloak, with the translucent greenstone pendant on her breast, she stood on the brink of the precipice and sang a song of love and longing for her unfaithful husband, a song which is still remembered by her people. Then she cast herself headlong to her death, preferring the shadowy underworlds to the poignant memories of her faithless husband.

On the western shore of the lake, near Moose Lodge, stands Pateko Island. It was used as an advanced observation post in inter-tribal wars, and had the reputation of being unconquered. It is now a burial ground for the descendants of a well known chief. On the eastern side of the island lived Mataura, a beneficent taniwha and protector of Ngati-Pikiao. When a famous chief died, Mataura was to be seen in the form of a huge tree floating on the lake.

The Okere Falls, where the Kaituna River enters Rotoiti, are overhung with tree ferns and forest trees. Tourists visit the River Cave, Hinemoa's Steps and the Trout Pool. Above the falls there was an old-time pa, which was the home of the famous chief Tutea. For many years the falls bore his name. At the foot of the falls was a taniwha who acted as watch dog for Tutea and warned him when his enemies were on the warpath. When he died, Tutea was buried in the cave underneath the Okere Falls.

The mountain Matawhauru is another of the many sacred mountains of Maoriland. We can catch a glimpse of the working of the Maori mind as we investigate this mountain. In spite of its height it cannot be seen from the sea-coast, and thus could not be used as a landmark for fishers in their canoes. For this reason its mana was great, for it did not serve men in their search for food.

Another sacred place was Onguru, near Kakanui, the site of the singing tree. The precipitous slopes were known as the cliff of wailing. When a new canoe was carved from a stately totara, it was taken to the cliff and propelled over the edge, so that it dropped from a considerable height into the water. If it survived the test, it was then put into use, for it would stand up to any storm that might

Onguru, the place of testing of canoes

rage on the lake. Much work was required in the making of a canoe, and the moments before the test were nerve-racking to all who had had a share in the construction. From their cries the cliff got its name.

The visitor to Rotoiti will not find Kuharua on the map, but in ancient times there grew on the shore at this place a conspicuous totara tree which first sprang from the headdress of the fabulous hero Hatupatu.

Many another legend has been told of Rotoiti. There is a spot on the shore which was famous for its boulders. When a feast was held in one of the kaingas or pas, and stones were needed for heating the huge ovens, they were always taken from this one place. They were round and convenient in size, but constant use had made them wary. The Maoris would visit the beach a day or two before the feast to make sure the stones were there. Then they would keep well away for a day or two, for the sensitive stones would suspect the motives of the visitors and hide beneath the sand. It was when they least expected it that they were seized and carried to the marae. There they were heated with fire, at the bottom of the holes dug in the earth, and covered with green leaves and fern fronds. The food was wrapped in leaves and placed on top, covered with more greenery and flax mats, watered liberally and finally covered with earth which was stamped hard. In this way the steam cooked the food perfectly. After the feast the stones were always returned to their place on the beach.

Finally, on our way to Rotoehu we come to the Wishing Tree, where many a white man and woman have stood and wished for some peculiarly pakeha request. But listen to the story of Hinehopu's Tree as it has come down to us through the lips of wise men and women in the whare runanga at night:

The story goes back to the beginning of Ngati-Pikiao

Hinehopu's Wishing Tree

history, indeed to the very days of Pikiao himself, who was descended from the famous Tama-te-kapua. Rakeiti bore many children to Pikiao, but alas, every one was a girl. Kawata-puarangi, father of Pikiao, often-times full of hope and many times disappointed, exclaimed, "When am I to have a male grandchild to lift my jaw to one side in my hour of need?" To Pikiao he said, "Take your favours elsewhere, my son. Leave your wife and go to the house of Ruaroa, and there you will find the line of male descent."

When Pikiao told Rakeiti the words of his father, she replied, "Continue to mate with me, my husband, as the river of Takapuhaia still flows."

But Kawata-puarangi's words had bitten deep into the heart of Pikiao. Heedless of his wife's prophecy that a son would be born to them, he left her and went to the

Hongi's warriors drag their canoes across the portage

country inhabited by the descendants of the *Tainui* canoe, and chose a woman of noble birth. Their first-born son was named Mahuta, later to become Maori King.

After a time Pikiao returned to Rakeiti. She at last bore him a son, who in turn grew up, married, and fathered Pikiao II, who married Hinehopu; and it is from this union that the Ngati-Pikiao people sprang. Hinehopu came from a people who were credited with supernatural powers and their gifts descended to her. By the tree where she met her husband, she called on the spirits of her forebears to make tapu the place of meeting; and from that time, say the Maori, the tree had the power of granting wishes, together with the equally potent gift of bringing misfortune on those who failed to make tribute to it.

Beware then, pakeha. Leave a fern frond or a sprig of leaves at the foot of Hinehopu's Wishing Tree, lest disaster overtake you on your journey past the lakes. And if there are white horses on the waves of Rotoiti, remember that you are seeing Hinehopu combing her hair.

Sun-dappled, a fairy glade in the forest, Hongi's Track is more than a motor highway. It is a graceful and entrancing gateway to wonderland. It is here, almost above all else in the thermal country, that one would expect to hear of tales of magic, of haunting patu-paiarehe, of the flute notes of romantic love. But legend is confined to Hinehopu's Wishing Tree.

Under the shadow of Matawhauru a grim scene comes back to us from a not-so-distant past. In the year 1823 Hongi, musket-armed Napoleon of the north, brought his war canoes to the Bay of Plenty. They stole up the Pongakawa stream to its headwaters and dragged their canoes overland to Rotoehu, and again from there, through more than a mile of dense forest, to the western shore of Rotoiti.

Across the pass of Tahuna the fierce warriors stealthily

manhandled the heavy canoes. They launched them on Rotoiti at Tapuaeharuru,* slipped through the Ohau Channel, and delivered a surprise attack on Mokoia Island. No right-minded, sensible man would have dreamed that such a feat could be successful, but under Hongi the blood-lusting Nga-Puhi achieved the impossible and the memory of their exploit lives in the name Hongi's Track, which replaced Tahuna Pass. This is not fable. It is stark history. If you cannot see the dark shapes of creeping canoes in these fairy glades at least you can see at Te Wairoa, the Buried Village, part of a canoe which took part in this fearful expedition.

*One translation of the name is "the marching feet of the multitude", but this implies "resounding footsteps", and we can be sure that Hongi's men stole like silent shadows down the beach.

Chapter Twelve

THE EASTERN LAKES

Rotoehu and Rotoma

OF ROTOEHU (turbid lake) and Rotoma (clear lake) few stories are told. Their history is shared with nearby Rotoiti. Cowan tells us of Kotiora, overlord of Rotoehu. On a raid against Ngati-Pikiao, Kotiora captured a young woman named Te Aoniwaho and carried her off as his wife.

It was a living death, for Kotiora was sadistic and overbearing. On one occasion Te Aoniwaho put a basket of whitebait in the steam oven, and when it was opened the food was not cooked. Kotiora would accept no excuse and demanded his morning kai without delay. Reluctantly Te Aoniwaho set the tiny fish before him. When he found that it was only half cooked, Kotiora fell into a rage. Seizing his wife roughly, he emptied the steaming food over her head. The girl fled to her whare, the tears streaming down her face, not on account of her physical anguish, but because of the deadly contempt shown in her husband's action, for to the Maori the head is tapu, sacred, and cooked food is unclean.

During the night she tip-toed from the whare, launched a small canoe and paddled up the western arm of Rotoehu. Then, careless of the goblins and haunting creatures of the night, she ran along the Tahuna trail. On the shores of Rotoiti she found another small canoe, and as the stars paled and the golden dawn flushed the sky, she reached the kainga which had been her girlhood home.

There was no need to incite her people to avenge the insult. Murder, rapine and abduction could be excused, but not this contemptuous treatment of a high-born woman of Ngati-Pikiao.

Messengers raced from kainga to kainga and, as darkness fell, canoes came from every village on Rotoiti, arrowing their way through the still waters to the beach of Tapuaeharuru. Bare feet padded quietly along the bush track. Before another dawn the men of Ngati-Pikiao rushed the sleeping village. Skulls split on the edge of the thirsty meres, and taiahas and tewhatewha drank deep as the morning light grew stronger.

Later in the day the victorious canoes returned and Kotiora was placed on the marae to listen to the account of his approaching death. Then came the death blow, and Kotiora was garnished and provided food for the satisfied people of Rotoiti.

And of course there was cause for a return visit from the warriors of Rotoehu, and again from Rotoiti, for that was the custom of the Maori people.

It is a grim story but it had a pleasing moral, as Cowan gave it: "Be kind to your Aoniwaho, even though you faint with hunger; deal leniently with her cookery.

Kotiora and his young wife

Restrain your gibes, hurl not her imperfect dishes at her. For the worm may turn; and her relatives may descend and rend you."*

Okataina

Okataina is a starfish of a lake, with long arms, tucked between Rotorua, Rotoiti and Tarawera. For centuries a place of teeming Maori activity, it was neglected for many years following the departure of its inhabitants to Rotorua to enjoy the amenities brought by the pakeha. In later years the lake has come into its own. "Surrounded by its high, steep, wooded hills," wrote Irma O'Connor, "it lies before us, shining with the unreal radiance of a dream, lit with the hidden fires of an opal, and so glassy still that every leaf and frond and tree, every tiny cloud overhead is reflected with crystal clearness, and we hold our breath in wonder, afraid to break the spell. This is beauty as God made it at the dawn of our island's story."

Before the coming of the white man, the lake was a connecting waterway between Rotoiti and Tarawera. As Hongi's men dragged their canoes overland from Rotoehu to Rotoiti, so in early years the warriors of Ngati-Pikiao did the same between Rotoiti and Okataina, and again between Okataina and Tarawera.

Round the shores of the lake every out-thrust peninsula was crowned by a fighting pa. One, appropriately named, was called "Island Projecting like a Tongue." Defiantly facing any foe was the pa of Te Koutu on the northern arm of the lake. Three hundred years ago it was commanded by the famous chief Te Rangi-takaroro. He made his tribe, the Ngati-Tarawhai, the scourge of the surrounding country. It is to him that we owe the present-day name

*Legends of the Maori, Pomare and Cowan, p. 196.

The laughter of Te Rangi-takaroro

of the lake. There was a rock, since submerged, where once Te Rangi rested for a while. Perhaps some joke was shared there with his warriors, perhaps some incident occurred which excited his laughter, for the rock was thereafter called the place of laughter. Later the name was transferred to the lake, which was known as Te Moana-i-kataina-a-Te-Rangi-takaroro (The Sea where Te Rangi-takaroro Laughed).

It has been suggested that, as a literal translation would be "The Sea at which Te Rangi-takaroro Laughed", his laughter was directed at the presumption shown at calling the little lake a sea! At least it may be said that Te Rangi enjoyed a gargantuan joke long ago, and though the jest was lost, the laughter remained, enshrined in the name Okataina (the place of laughter).

Chapter Thirteen

THE STORY OF HATUPATU

THE ROAD TO TE WAIROA leads south-west from Rotorua and skirts the shores of the Blue and Green Lakes, with a branch curling across the hills to lovely Okareka. The old Maori track to Te Wairoa (the Buried Village) crossed the pass of Pareuru and there are to be seen the claw-marks of Kura-ngaituku, the ogre bird-woman of a celebrated legend.

The story of Hatupatu and the bird-woman can be traced through many of the famous places of the Rotorua district, and it is at this point, where the evidence of Hatupatu's narrow escape is engraved in the rock, that we may recall the famous story.

It was long ago, in the time of Ihenga, that Hatupatu's mother and father brought him and his brothers to Rotorua. They settled in the village on Mokoia Island by the lake-side. One day Hanui and Haroa and their young brother went bird-snaring in the forests between Lakes Taupo and Rotorua, and there they had good hunting. They built themselves a shelter to live in, and a store house where they kept the birds they had killed. Each night they plucked and cooked them and preserved them in their own fat in calabashes. Hanui and Haroa were great hunters, but Hatupatu was so small that he was not allowed to join in the hunt, but had to stay in the hut, where he had to do the common work of a slave. Like a slave, he had to live on the scraps left over from his brothers' meals. Hatupatu resented this treatment, but his brothers were so much stronger than he that he could do nothing about it.

As the days went by he grew thinner, and the thinner he grew, the more desperate he became. One morning he could stand it no longer. As soon as his brothers were safely out of the way, he raided the storehouse and ate the choicest birds until he could eat no more. Having satisfied his hunger, he looked round the storehouse and felt alarmed. There was no doubt that his brothers would notice how many birds had been eaten, but he had a plan which would allay their suspicions. He scattered the remaining calabashes round the shelter and trampled a number of times the muddy path that led to it. Taking one of the spears he ran it into himself in several places and bruised his face and then, as he heard his brothers' voices, he lay down on the floor of the hut and groaned realistically. His brothers lent over him and asked him what had happened. Hatupatu groaned again and whispered that the encampment had been raided by a war party, which had taken some of the potted birds, and though he had defended them valiantly, he had been wounded and left for dead. While Hanui inspected the damage, Haroa melted some of the bird fat and poured it over the cuts that Hatupatu had inflicted on himself and made him comfortable. They were a little puzzled that only a few of the birds had been taken, but they had no suspicion of their brother. Once the excitement had worn off they took no further notice of him and Hatupatu was left to brood on the further side of the fire. His brothers ate their fill and neglected Hatupatu, but his skin was so tight that he could not have swallowed another morsel. That was the Maori habit — to eat to repletion while the food was there, for who could tell where the next meal was to come from.

But the fullest meal will not last for ever. A few days later Hatupatu was as hungry as ever. "That throat of yours can swallow anything," says an old proverb, and Hatupatu put it to the proof. His stratagem had been so successful that he thought it worth repeating. On a second occasion it worked, and on a third, but by this time the brothers were becoming suspicious. Hatupatu was too young to realise that his devices were becoming transparent.

As he sat outside the storehouse cramming handfuls of succulent flesh into his mouth, Hanui and Haroa appeared in front of him. After leaving the shelter, they had hidden in the forest and had watched to see what Hatupatu would do. There was no mercy in their hearts for their younger brother. Enraged at his deceitfulness, they rushed at him and killed him with a blow and hid his body under a pile of feathers.

Their hunting expedition was nearly at an end. A few more days and the calabashes were full, and they returned to their home at Rotorua. The first question their mother asked when they arrived was, "Where is Hatupatu?"

"We don't know. We haven't seen him for a while."

THE STORY OF HATUPATU

It was not a convincing reply. "You must know where he is," their father said sternly. "He went away with you and he hasn't come back. It was your responsibility to look after him."

"Hatupatu left us many days ago while we were out hunting," they maintained stubbornly. "When we found that he had gone we assumed that he had left for home."

"Did you look for him? He might have had an accident in the forest and could have died because you did not look for him. Surely you could have come home to make sure? You always treated him like a slave."

His sons had nothing to say. Anger mounted within their father like a rising tide. "It was not neglect," he said slowly. "I can see it now. You have killed your brother!"

Sorrow came upon the village. The parents mourned their son. Hatupatu's father had skill in magic, and he decided to send a spirit to seek for his youngest son. This spirit was found in the body of Tamumu-ki-te-rangi, the blowfly (He who Buzzes in the Sky). Tamumu buzzed to good purpose, flying above the treetops until he came to the clearing where the brothers had camped. He flew down first to the hut, then to the storehouse, and finally to a great heap of feathers from the plucked birds. He flew round and round and great power went out from his tiny body, until the feathers stirred and slipped down from the pile as Hatupatu stood upright, his wounds healed. Tamumu flew joyfully away. Hatupatu was not sure what had happened to him, but at least he had learned that the camp was not a healthy place for him. He took up a spear that his brothers had left behind, and with new assurance entered the forest. He was travelling in the direction of home.

As he walked along a narrow track a bird flew through the trees. A moment later it was impaled on Hatupatu's

The rock where Hatupatu hid from the ogress

spear — and also on the sharp-pointed lips of Kura-ngaituku. His spear fell from nerveless fingers, for Hatupatu had come face to face with the dreaded bird-woman, an ogress with long talons, spreading wings and lips that could pierce like a sharpened spear. He turned and ran for his life, but Kura-ngaituku's wings carried her quickly through the trees. A moment later he was held firmly in her claws and carried to her home.

Hatupatu stayed there for a long time, in great discomfort. The house was full of tame lizards and birds and it was evident that Kura-ngaituku intended to add him to her collection of pets. Food seemed to become an obsession with the young man, for he was continually hungry. The bird-woman ate her food raw and offered uncooked meat to her charge, but Hatupatu was revolted by it. Every

THE STORY OF HATUPATU

now and again she went hunting and in her absence the boy searched for a way of escape, but the eyes of the birds and lizards followed his every move.

When the birds in the neighbourhood became scarce, Hatupatu encouraged his gaoler to go further afield.

"You had better go a long way today," he said. "Go to the first range of hills, to the second range of hills, to the tenth range, to the hundredth, to the thousandth range."

Kura-ngaituku went off early in the morning, and as soon as she was out of sight, Hatupatu satisfied his hunger. Taking the ogress's weapon, he killed the birds and lizards — all except one bird, which hid from him and escaped when Hatupatu opened the door.

Hatupatu ran in the opposite direction, happy in the knowledge that the bird-woman would have difficulty in finding him. But the escaped bird soon found his mistress and reported that Hatupatu had fled. Kura-ngaituku lifted her sharp-pointed head and sniffed the breeze. She spread her wings and with long, steady strokes the miles were soon eaten up. Far away Hatupatu heard the flapping of wings and a low chant which grew louder and louder. "Step out, stretch along; step out, stretch along; I'll catch you there now, Hatupatu; I'll catch you there now, Hatupatu."

In a panic the boy rushed to a rock that stood above the fern and chanted magic words: "O rock, open for me, open, open." The rock obediently opened, revealing a cavity that hid him, and closed again as he entered. The traveller of today may stop on the Taupo-Putaruru highway and see standing by the roadside the rock with the cavity in which Hatupatu hid. If he is of a romantic disposition he may place an offering of fern or leaves there which, because of the ancient power of the gods, may very well protect him from the taniwha and ogres that lie in wait for the motorist of the twentieth century.

The death of the bird-woman

THE STORY OF HATUPATU

Hatupatu waited until the sound of wings had died away. He crept out and made his way hurriedly towards his home. It must have been as he fetched a wide circuit and crossed the pass of Pareuru that his pursuer caught up with him, and there her claw marks were preserved in the rock for all time.

Fear and the thought of home and safety so close at hand gave winged feet to Hatupatu. He rushed down the hillside towards the boiling fumeroles and shuddering mud pools of Whakarewarewa. The bird-woman had never been there before. Hatupatu gave a mighty leap which carried him across a boiling pool. In her ignorance Kurangaituku began to wade across it, not dreaming that the water was boiling, and so she perished and Hatupatu escaped.

Arriving at the edge of the lake he dived into the water and came up the beach by his home on Mokoia Island. He soaked himself in a warm pool and lay there until a slave came down from the village. He seized hold of him and said, "I am Hatupatu. Tell me, where are my parents?"

The old slave gasped. "Are you really alive, Hatupatu? Is it indeed you?"

"It is I. Are my brothers at my father's home?"

"No," the old slave said. "There has been bad feeling between them, for your parents thought you had been killed by your brothers. Since then they have lived by themselves."

When Hatupatu entered his parents' whare, tears of joy fell freely. "We must be quiet," Hatupatu said as he embraced them. "Quiet, lest my brothers hear."

He said this because he could see that his parents were frightened of the older brothers. "Let me hide in the cave where the kumaras are stored," he said.

Before it was light, he was smuggled into the kumara

cave, and his parents said nothing of his arrival. Every day, when no one was looking, Hatupatu's mother smuggled the best food to her favourite son, but it was not long before the other brothers noticed that they were having a plain diet. Being noisy, quarrelsome young men, they showed their disapproval and treated both their parents and the slaves roughly.

Hatupatu remained in hiding. His experiences during the past week had taught him wisdom, and in the darkness of the cave he prepared an unpleasant time for his older brothers.

Somehow the news got round the village that Hatupatu had returned, and it was whispered from one to another until the brothers, who terrorised the pa, heard of it. "What nonsense," they said. "Hatupatu is dead."

"How do you know that he is dead?" their father demanded quickly. "According to what you told us, he returned home. It seems to me that you know a good deal more than you pretend."

"It is no business of yours, old man," they said.

"If Hatupatu were here he would defend his father's honour."

His sons laughed coarsely. "Let Hatupatu learn to defend himself before he takes on other responsibilities!"

Nevertheless the young warriors were uneasy. They knew that Hatupatu was dead, but the rumours of his return were persistent and, to be on the safe side, they armed themselves.

It was not long before they realised that the impossible had happened and that Hatupatu had been seen. "Where? Where is he?" they demanded.

"Down by the kumara pit." The brothers rushed there, brandishing their two-handed swords, while the whole

Hatupatu comes out of his hiding place to face his brothers

population of the village followed to see what would happen.

Hanui and Haroa recoiled in alarm. The proud chief who came out of the store pit was not the little brother whom they had treated so scornfully. Black and white huia feathers garlanded his head and in his ears were bunches of soft white down from the stomach of the albatross. His cloak glowed in the sunshine with the red feathers of the kaka, but the light in his eyes gleamed even more brightly. He swung his wooden battle-axe round his head as he advanced towards his brothers.

Recovering from their surprise, the young warriors rushed at their brother in an attempt to take him off guard, but Hatupatu was ready for them. He stood his ground until he was nearly in reach of their flailing weapons. Hatupatu lifted his own battle-axe and calmly deflected his brothers' weapons. Then he sprang into action. Only the sunshine gleaming on the polished wood marked its passage as the tewhatewha sang through the air, felling the two who had always hated him. Karika, another brother who came to their aid, was as easily knocked over and disarmed by a swift parry with the handle of Hatupatu's weapons. In the moment of time that elapses as the shadow of a bird sweeps over the ground, the boasting toas were reduced and the fight knocked out of them.

For Hatupatu it was the day of atonement for all the indignities he had suffered, and no less for his father. "Oh, my sons," he said, "you have been strong against the weak. Would that the gods had given you the same courage in facing foemen who are worthy of your valour! You have ill-treated your young brother and boasted of your strength. Now that he has attained the stature of a man you have been humbled. It is I, your father, who speak to you now, with a boldness that has been conferred on me by my youngest son. Be men! Show your strength in a more fitting way by avenging the wrongs of Te Arawa.

"Do you not remember the indignities we suffered when Raumati set fire to our ancestral canoe? That wrong has never been avenged. Now is your opportunity to recover your lost mana, the mana that has been lost at the hand of my last-born child."

Hanui, Haroa and Karika felt the sting of his words. In silence they made their preparations for war, lest they be shamed in the eyes of their tribe. It was only when they were accompanied by their henchmen and launched the war canoes that they recovered and boasted of the revenge they would take on the people of Raumati. With something like their old self-confidence they brandished their paddles and sent the war canoes surging into the waters of the lake.

Hatupatu watched their departure. While his brothers had been preparing for the campaign his father had taught him the pattern of Raumati's moko, the tattoo of the face, by which the adversary could be recognised. He waited until his brothers were well away from the shore and then, the legends tell us, he gathered up thirty cloaks of red feathers, put them over his arm, and plunged into the lake. Swimming strongly under water, he came to a bed of mussels and ate them. On again to the lake shore, where he spread the cloaks out to dry and waited for the canoes to arrive.

"Where is your canoe? How did you get here?" his brothers asked as soon as they landed, but Hatupatu shrugged his shoulders and threw the chaplet of leaves which he had been weaving on the ground, where they took root and eventually grew into a grove of sturdy pohutukawa trees. After the canoes had left, Hatupatu

Hatupatu's army of warriors

pursued them to Lake Rotoiti, where he repeated his former actions and was responsible for planting a stand of totaras.

The war-party left their canoes and marched quickly to the coast of Maketu, where they engaged their enemies. The war-party was divided into three groups, each under the command of one of the brothers. In spite of his recent prowess there was no place in the taua* for Hatupatu. He went his own way. Choosing a strategic position, he went to sleep. Early the following morning, before it was light, he tied many bushes together with flax, and covered them with the red feather cloaks he had brought with him. From a distance they looked like warriors, and the deception was completed when the wind blew from the land and set the bushes bending and swaying.

*War-party.

THE STORY OF HATUPATU

As the sun rose Hatupatu watched his brothers. As soon as they had finished exhorting their warriors, who had taken up a position at some distance, Hatupatu, bravely clad and with his hair tied in four knots surmounted by the feathers of a rangatira, strode backwards and forwards addressing his mock war-party. He stood up as though inspecting them and disappeared behind the bushes. Bending down, he undid his hair, leaving only one top-knot above his forehead, changed his cloak for another of a different colour, and came forward once more to inspect his "men".

He made several lightning changes, thus giving the impression of a stalwart band of warriors led by a number of outstanding chiefs. Hatupatu's intention was not to deceive his brothers. He knew that a little farther off every action was being watched by the enemy. They felt capable of repulsing the assaults of the war-party, but Hatupatu's performance made their hearts quail. Never before had they seen a small war-party commanded by so many young chiefs, and they feared that the pick of the warriors might still be in hiding.

They had no time for further thought. The warriors of Hanui, Haroa and Karika launched themselves at the enemy. But Raumati's men were hardened in battle. The spears flew through the air like birds and when the rain of death was over and the battle was fought hand to hand, the experienced warriors of Raumati had the better of their assailants. They pressed them back slowly, until the faint-hearted of the Arawas turned and fled. Nothing then could save them — nothing except the greater guile of Hatupatu.

During the conflict it appeared as though his warriors were sitting down watching the progress of the battle. When the rout of Arawa began, Hatupatu jumped to his

The gift of the head of Raumati

feet and ran to face the victorious warriors of Raumati. At first he was hidden by a fold in the ground, and when he emerged and sprang towards them, they had no doubt that in a moment his taua would thunder across the rise and attack their flank. "Turn on them, drive them back," Hatupatu shouted as they paused, and his rallying cry halted his fleeing tribesmen. They looked back and saw Hatupatu rushing towards the thickest press of the enemy, brandishing his battle-axe. A moment later he was lost to sight, but the bodies of men fell like trees in a gale and, though they caught no glimpse of Hatupatu, they saw the blade of his battle-axe rising and falling like the adze head of a tree-feller.

The men of Arawa rallied to the young warrior's cry and soon the tide of battle flowed strongly and the enemy

THE STORY OF HATUPATU

were put to rout. While they were occupied Hatupatu sought their old enemy Raumati and, when he recognised him by the moko which his father had described so carefully, he cut off his head and concealed it under his cloak.

When the battle was over, the ovens were lit and the bodies of the enemy cooked and eaten. Te Arawa returned in triumph to Rotorua, bearing the smoked heads of the men of Raumati as grim trophies of their victory.

"Who has brought me the head of Raumati that I may rejoice in the righting of an ancient wrong?" their chief asked as the canoes ground to a standstill on the beach of Mokoia.

One after the other, Hanui, Haroa and Karika displayed the heads of slain warriors, but when all three had been shown, the old man's head sank on his breast.

"Alas! Raumati has escaped!"

All this time Hatupatu had been in the background, but at his father's words he came forward and held out the head of their enemy. His father's eyes lit up. He dropped his cloak and entered the lake waters to give praise to the gods who had favoured his youngest son.

And, as the wise men tell us, Hatupatu was raised to honour in the tribe, but Hanui, Haroa and Karika were debased.

Captain Gilbert Mair has told other stories of this famous warrior. He says that Hatupatu overtook Raumati at Maunganui in Tauranga Harbour. Raumati had attempted to escape by swimming to Matakana Island. Hatupatu finally caught up with him at the north spit, and it was there that he severed his head, calling the place Panepane (the severed head).

Reference has been made elsewhere to the trees that have grown from the chaplet of Hatupatu, and this is where fiction perhaps borders on fact. After a raid on the tribe of Te Kawerau, Hatupatu saw a totara tree growing on Haroharo Hill. He put a twig from the tree in his hair, and later planted it on Mokoia Island. Further up the hill, in the sacred grove, he planted a single tawa tree, and from Katikati he brought a puriri tree to the island.

Captain Mair claimed that Hatupatu was the pioneer of acclimatisation in Rotorua. With some imagination and thought for the future, the warrior experimented in introducing eels which his slaves had caught in the Pukerimu and Oraka streams on the Tokoroa Plains. The slaves packed the eels in damp moss and brought them alive to Ohinemutu. These experiments were viewed with some suspicion by the tohunga of Ruapeka pa, who told Hatapatu that unless the fish were put under a spell they would never be recaptured. Following his instructions some dry fern was placed close to the shore and burnt, and as the karakia were pronounced the eels were placed in the hot ashes. Although they wriggled quickly to the water, they were scorched by the heat. Several days later they died and floated to the surface, thus providing a meal for the tohunga of Ohinemutu. When Hatupatu heard what had happened, the tohunga had little time to enjoy his meal. He was dispatched much more quickly than the eels.

Hatupatu later brought fish called koaro from Rotoaira, south of Taupo. These flourished in Rotorua and Rotoiti. Mair stated that the koaro were blind, but that after living in the lakes for a while they recovered their sight. They flourished until trout were introduced to the lakes, when the flashing Rainbows and browns evidently found them a succulent dish.

Hatupatu's most ambitious project was an attempt at the introduction of snapper from the Bay of Plenty. A hundred slaves were stationed at intervals along the track from Maketu to Rotorua, each slave holding a calabash filled

THE STORY OF HATUPATU

with salt water. Seventy snapper were caught at Maketu and these were placed carefully in a watertight vessel made of totara bark. As the precious parcel of living fish was hurried to Rotorua the salt water was replenished from the calabashes on the way; but by the time the party reached Ohau, only one gigantic fish remained alive. It was immediately placed in the water, where it swam to Mokoia and circled the island with its tail projecting from the water. This was a bad omen which was promptly fulfilled, for the fish swam to the place where it had been liberated and gasped out its life in the shallows of the fresh water lake.

A final experiment was with crayfish, which again were brought from Maketu. At first it seemed that this bold experiment had been unsuccessful, for nothing further was seen of these koura. Some months later as a travelling party was journeying from the coast at night, they reached a place called Te Hiapo. One of the Maoris stumbled over an object on the track, and cried out in alarm that he had been wounded. Torches were brought and it was discovered that he had trodden on a huge koura. The place was then named Koura-tara-mamae (the painful wound from a crayfish spear).

Truly the imaginative Hatupatu has a claim to fame in the legends of Rotorua.

Chapter Fourteen

THE BLUE AND GREEN LAKES

Lake Tikitapu

Hatupatu's story has taken us far from the road that leads to the twin lakes of Tikitapu and Rotokakahi. First we come to Tikitapu, the lake of blue waters, divided by the high ridge which was known as Te Ahi-manawa — the place where the heart was cooked. Many years ago a sorcerer was caught on this ridge, standing naked before his altar fire, in the very act of chanting his evil incantations. He was slain and his body eaten, but his heart was offered to the god Maru on his own altar fire.

The contrasting colour of the waters of the adjacent lakes will always fascinate those who see them, yet it is said that in the dawn of time a famous log drifted on both lakes, passing from one to the other through a subterranean passage. They are lakes of mystery and enchantment, and first we must tell the story of Kataore, the monster of Tikitapu.

In his young days this monster taniwha lived at Rotoehu, was quiet and well-mannered and had become something of a pet to the people there. Being of an adventurous disposition, he migrated to Lake Tikitapu and was welcomed by a chief who lived on the western shore in a gully under the shadow of Moerangi. A pet taniwha was a novelty, for the Rotorua district was noted for the ravages of these legendary beasts of prey. Kataore was harmless and was seldom seen, for the well-trodden track between Te Wairoa and Rotorua was on the eastern shore of the lake, far removed from Moerangi, where Kataore had his lair.

Some years after the taniwha came to Tikitapu, disturbing rumours began to spread abroad. There were mysterious disappearances as lonely travellers passed by the lake on their way to or from Rotorua. And indeed there was cause for alarm. Like many another young and lovable animal, Kataore's nature had changed as he grew up. Silently he would steal through the forest, and as the traveller passed the lake and entered the forest path where the trees met overhead and a dim green light filtered through the leafy canopy, the taniwha crept silently between the trees. With a single gulp of its cavernous jaws the traveller would disappear into its capacious maw. For a little while the birds would cease their singing, until the satisfied monster crept back to its lair on the sides of Moerangi.

Suspicion crystallised into certainty. The enraged tribespeople of Tarawera, Okareka, Te Wairoa and Rotorua determined on action when they heard the sad fate of the high-born Tuhi-karaparapa, who, on her way from Tarawera to Ohinemutu to marry the young chief Reretoi,

The tohungas chant a karakia to overcome the taniwha

was overtaken by the monster near the lake and devoured. At last Kataore had over-reached himself. He had swallowed the chief's daughter and several of her attendants, but others escaped and spread the news of the disaster.

Reretoi was overcome with grief, but the lust for vengeance burned strongly in his breast. At his call there rallied to his aid the 140 bold warriors who had already assisted in the destruction of the taniwha Pekehaua at Te Awahou, and other monsters of the hot lakes. They quickly formed a war-party and marched to Tikitapu, skirting the lake and arriving at the slopes of Moerangi.

There was much debate amongst the members of the avenging party that night, but before they went to sleep the plan of attack had been decided. At the first light of dawn the tohungas who accompanied the expedition chanted the sacred karakia that had power against all taniwha. While they were at their work the others gathered flax and plaited strong ropes.

As the sun rose higher they could see the darker shape of a cave on the precipitous mountain side. "It must be there that the monster has his lair," Reretoi exclaimed. As one man they crept cautiously forward and took up a position close to the mouth of the cave. It was very still, and above the murmuring of the waves on the beach below and the sound of the fluttering fantails among the trees, they heard a deep, muffled breathing.

"It must be Kataore," Reretoi whispered in the ear of his friend Pikata. Yes, this was Pikata the taniwha-slayer who had descended with the trap into the cold waters of Awahou. Taking the nooses of the ropes in their hands the two young men crept into the cave, while their friends held firmly to the other end. Once inside they peered into the darkness. At first they could see nothing but two

The search for the lost tiki of the Blue Lake

bright circles of light like incandescent greenstone. These were the eyes of Kataore, gleaming like fire, but his body was still and the fearful spines that ran along his back drooped down his scaly flanks. The incantations of the tohungas had sapped the taniwha's power.

Reretoi and Pikata advanced cautiously and managed to slip the nooses over the vast head. Running lightly, they sprang through the cave entrance. As they appeared, the young men hauled on the ropes. They took the strain, drawing the taniwha out of the cave, quickly at first and then more slowly. Kataore was roused. The spines were erected and the very air seemed to quiver with his roaring. It was enough to make the stoutest warrior quail, but Reretoi and Pikata's one hundred and forty were chosen men. They wound the ropes round the tree trunks and pulled the nooses tightly round the monster's neck. Presently his strength began to fail and the murderous blows of his great tail grew feeble. At a signal some of the men sprang forward and attacked Kataore with mere, tewhatewha and kotiate until the life went out of him and he lay prone amongst the battered trees.

With sharp cutting tools of bone and greenstone they stripped his flesh, some of which was cooked at once, and the rest potted and distributed amongst the tribes which had suffered from his depredations, while the pitiful remains of those he had swallowed were buried. His heart was cut out and cooked and eaten by the tohungas between the Blue and Green Lakes, on the ridge Te Ahi-manawa.

That is the story of Kataore, the scourge of Tikitapu. It is a tale of bloodshed and strife and sorrow which continued long after his death, for the joy of the victorious war-party from Ohinemutu was matched only by the sorrow of Tangaroa-mihi, the owner of Kataore. The taniwha had always deceived his owner, pretending to be docile and affectionate, and Tangaroa believed that the slaying of his defenceless taniwha was an act of aggression which could be wiped out only by long and bloody warfare against Te Arawa.

There is another half-forgotten tale of the Blue Lake which is enshrined in its name — Tikitapu — the sacred greenstone neck ornament. It is a story far removed from uncanny memories of taniwha . . . just the simple tale of the daughter of a high-born chief, who swam in the lake and lost a treasured heirloom looped through a flax cord and hung round her neck. What frenzied searching there must have been for the loss of that hallowed possession, the sacred tiki of her tribe. The blue waters of Tikitapu still hide the tikitapu that was lost so long ago.

The island of Motutawa

LAKE ROTOKAKAHI

We cross the ridge Te Ahi-manawa and look down on the contrasting waters of Rotokakahi, as green as Tikitapu is blue. The name is more prosaic, but a reminder that these deserted shores were once thickly populated. The lake was noted for its kakahi, the delicious shellfish found in large quantities on the sandy bed. Rotokakahi means the lake of the shellfish kakahi. It was an important part of the diet of the lake dwellers, eaten raw, underdone or well-cooked. It was a favourite food for invalids and, strangely enough, for motherless babies when a wet-nurse was not available. The shellfish was cooked and softened with the water in the shell, so that it could be sucked like milk. "Ko te kakahi te whaea o te tamaiti," they said (The kakahi is the mother of the child).

THE BLUE AND GREEN LAKES

The round island of Motutawa in the southern arm of the lake was famous in ancient history. It was occupied by a hapu of the Tuhourangi tribe, who now live at Whakarewarewa. But light and laughter have long ceased on the tapu island, where the bones of Hinemoa and many others lie buried. More than a hundred years ago a party of Nga-Puhi from the far north were massacred on the island. When the news reached the Bay of Islands it led to the startling descent of Hongi's warriors and the capture of the even more famous island of Mokoia in Rotorua.

Still later the old pa at Kaiteriria on the shore of the lake became the headquarters of the Arawa Constabulary Force under the command of Captain Gilbert Mair.

CHAPTER FIFTEEN

TARAWERA AND THE ERUPTION

THE CATACLYSM OF 1886, when Mount Tarawera erupted and devastated a vast area of country, is a major event in New Zealand history. In the present book we are concerned only with Maori legend, but some of the events of that fateful night occurred on the borders of witchcraft and magic.

TE WAIROA — THE BURIED VILLAGE

It was at Te Wairoa that we see most clearly the evidence of the appalling devastation that occurred on the night of June 10, 1886. The hand of nature covers the scars made by the titanic underground forces, and in the course of time the tiny Lake Rotomahana, which grew thirty-fold in size, appears ageless as the surrounding hills; but in Te Wairoa, the little village which was once a busy overnight stopping place for travellers on their way to see the wonders of the Pink and White Terraces, the remains of buried buildings can still be seen. Once upon a time it was a peaceful village in a pleasant setting of green; then for a time it was an ugly mud-covered waste; today the former beauty of the valley is restored and it preserves the memory for all time of that night of terror and destruction.

In one of these huts lived Tuhoto, the aged tohunga of Te Wairoa. He had seen his people's standards decline as they came under the influence of the pleasure-loving pakeha. As the days passed he withdrew himself more and more from the communal life of the kainga. He prayed to the gods of his people and his prayers were answered when Tamaohoi, the buried atua of Mount Tarawera, burst his bonds and scattered the molten rock and boiling mud over Te Wairoa, Moura, Te Ariki, and many another place, until seven Europeans and over a hundred Maoris were killed. As the destructive rain of stone and mud settled in a thick fall on Te Wairoa, Tuhoto's tiny whare was buried from sight.

Day succeeded day and the 100-year-old tohunga lay quiet in the dark tomb of his house. Immediately after the eruption rescue parties were organised in Rotorua, and the dangerous task of seeking for survivors was begun. Surely Tuhoto had paid for his curse that had blighted the green countryside! Yet when the searchers uncovered his whare, the old man was still alive. He remained protected by the roof, which saved him from the crushing weight of volcanic debris. At least that is what the white man says. The Maoris maintained that Tamaohoi had protected his tohunga and in that was the final proof of the wizard's responsibility for the eruption.

Tuhoto was taken to Rotorua and cared for by the pakeha, so that in spite of his hundred years he might have lived on. But for all his science and his pretended know-

The overwhelming of Te Wairoa

ledge, the pakeha is a foolish fellow. He would insist on cutting the old man's matted hair, and as it fell his life left his frail body, and the tohunga of Te Wairoa died.

Tarawera

Lake and mountain had long been places of mystery. Tuhoto of Te Wairoa, for all his power, would have been helpless if it had not been for the unearthly manifestations of the lake and its brooding mountain. Tuhoto could interpret the omens, but the secret of Tarawera's strength went back to the days of the *Arawa* canoe. Tamaohoi was an atua, a man-eating ogre who lived on the flanks of the mountain. As the thermal regions were occupied by the growing tribes of Te Arawa, unwary travellers were snatched and devoured by Tamaohoi.

When the news of these ambushes reached Ngatoro, the far-travelled tohunga who had climbed the bare heights of Tongariro and who summoned the fire gods of Hawaiki, he made a special expedition to Tarawera. The atua had no resistance to offer the skilled tohunga of Te Arawa. Ngatoro ascended the mountain and stamped with his foot until a huge chasm was formed. Into this pit he thrust the cannibal demon, covering him with the solid rock of the mountain.

Tamaohoi lay sleeping through the centuries until Tuhoto's prayers, or simply the passage of time, woke him from his long slumbers. There came the night when he rose and burst the mountain and laid waste all the land that lay at his feet.

In the meantime other events occurred which added to the tapu of Tarawera. Let us think of Tuhourangi, nine feet in height, great-great-great-grandson of the ariki Tama-te-kapua. He was one of the eight children of Rangitiki. At his death he was carried by his brothers a distance

The burial of Tuhourangi

of twenty miles, to the very summit of Ruawahia, one of the peaks of Tarawera, and there buried in a manner that befitted his position. From this great feat there came the oft-repeated saying, "the Arawa of the eight pulsating hearts". Each of these children bequeathed his name to an important sub-tribe of Te Arawa.

Then there was the Taniwha's Rock, now buried deep beneath the waters of Lake Tarawera. It was a shrine where voyagers made offerings to preserve them from the depredations of a dreaded monster of the lake.

And there was Matarewhawha, the floating log which rose and fell in the water, and one day was pulled ashore by a pakeha and burnt. Who could wonder that evil befell the dwellers by the shores of Lake Tarawera?

Mention must be made, also, of the phantom canoe, the wakawairua which was a portent of death to all who saw it. Its last appearance was only a few days before the eruption, when it was seen by pakeha as well as Maori.

The apparition was widely discussed amongst the Maoris and was reported to the tohunga Tuhoto.

"What does the canoe mean? Is it an omen?" he was asked.

"*He tohu tera, ara ka horo katoa tenei takiwa,*" he replied (It is an omen; it is a sign that all this region will be overwhelmed). And that saying was remembered by the Maori.

But perhaps after all Tuhoto was guiltless. It may be that he had no connection with the atua Tamaohoi and that the eruption was caused by men of Te Ariki who were foolish enough to disregard the sacredness of the mountain. This story was told by the famous guide Sophia and recorded by E. I. Massey in *The Tarawera Eruption 1886 and Some Maori Legends.*

"Now on Tarawera mountain, lady, there was a quantity of honey made by the wild bees. No one ought to have touched it, as everything there was tabooed (sacred and forbidden); but some young Maori men went up the mountain and took the honey, filling up billies (tin pots with covers) and other vessels with it; and they brought it all away to Te Ariki, and some to Rotomahana, where they gave it to the old chief Rangihehuwa, who lived at the foot of the Pink Terrace. Now I was going to guide my visitors round the Terraces, and when we landed from the boats I saw the old chief Rangihehuwa, and he offered me some of the honey; but I said, 'No, thank you,' for I knew it was tabooed; therefore it would be wrong to take it. For had not the two wise old men of my tribe shown me over the mountain when I first came to Tarawera from the Bay of Islands, and did we not see Tamahoe's* cave, and in it his big comb with which he used to comb his hair? It was lying on a stone in the cave. And did not the old men with

*Tamaohoi, the atua who was buried by Ngatoro-i-rangi.

The phantom canoe of Lake Tarawera

white hair tell me that everything on Tarawera was taboo? So I had not forgotten their warning, and when Rangihehuwa wanted me to take this honey, I said 'No.' I would not have it or let my people take it either, for I knew the danger, so would have nothing to do with it. Yes — I knew.

"Lady, it is strange but true, every one of those people that ate of the tabooed honey, every soul, perished in the eruption of Tarawera, that took place very soon after; but I and my people, who did not touch it, were all saved; and so we came safely and thankfully out of the great disaster of 1886."

Enough! The mountain was tapu. The tapu was destroyed and many lost their lives.

The wise pakeha, with the wisdom that comes after the

event, has often said that the Maori knew very well of the danger of the mountain. Tarawera, he says, means burnt peak, and what more appropriate name could one find for the fire-devastated summit of the brooding mountains? But literal interpretations of names can be misleading. Tara means spear as well as peak, for it is the name for sharp-pointed objects. More correctly it is to a bundle of bird-spears that Tarawera owes its name. Many years ago a chief from Hawke's Bay travelled overland until he came to the slope of the sinister mountain, where he built a shelter for himself. After a successful bird-hunting season on the forested slopes, he returned home, leaving his spears behind him. He came back a year later, only to find that his hut and the bird spears had been destroyed by fire, and it is to this incident that the mountain owes its name.

Rotomahana

Of the weird steaming waters of Rotomahana and the mysterious valley of Waimangu, legend has little to say. It needs no folk-lore, for recent years have provided more wonders than primitive man could imagine. Before the eruption of Tarawera, this "warm lake" was not more than 200 acres in extent, connected with Lake Tarawera by the Kaiwaka Stream (Eater of Canoes). At the time of the eruption the pleasant little lake with its two small islands was blown into the sky, and a vast crater, full of furious mud pools and geysers, took its place.

Gradually the winter rains filled the basin and formed a lake six miles in length and nearly thirty times the size of the little lake of earlier days. Its surface has risen too, and deep beneath the boiling waters which hiss and surge on the steaming cliffs of Hape-o-toroa, lies all that remains of the glistening stepped pools of the Pink Terraces. Long

The little islands in Lake Rotomahana

ago these world-renowned silica terraces were crowned by the boiling fountain Otu-kapua-rangi (Cloud of Heaven), while on the far side of the lake their beauty was challenged by the gleaming White Terraces.

That must be our parting memory of the hot lakes. There are vicious spurting pools of mud, swirling steam and sulphurous vapours which come straight from the frightening home of the god of volcanoes and subterranean fire, but delicate green ferns line the bubbling waters, blue waves lap against many-coloured terraces shining in the sun, and beauty is everywhere. Beauty, not only in the forested hills and the restless waves of the necklace of lakes, but in the minds of men who created so many stories to explain Wai-ora-a-Tane — the living water of the forest god.

Chapter Sixteen

PLACE NAMES OF THE THERMAL REGION

The following list contains the names of streams, geysers, lakes, hills, bays and other natural features of the thermal country. Where the origins of the names are known, they have been supplied. In such cases a full account of the circumstances of the naming has been given in the text of the book. Where the Maori name is reasonably plain, the meaning has been supplied, and is prefaced by an acknowledgement that it is a literal translation. This information may be of interest to readers, but it must be emphasised that a literal translation can be misleading, and is of little use to the serious student. In many cases, no attempt has been made to find a meaning, sometimes because the name may have been changed or corrupted, sometimes because there are many alternatives from which to make a choice.

Further information about the places will be found in the text of the book, and the relative page numbers are given. This list is therefore an index as well as a gazetteer.

ALADDIN'S CAVE: a cave with brightly coloured alum rock walls, at Orakei Korako.
ALUM CLIFFS: at Waiotapu. A descriptive name.
ALUM CREEK: drains Arikikapakapa Lake. A descriptive name. The Maori name is Waimangeao.
ANAPUTA: on the south shore of Lake Rotoiti. Lit. *to pass through the cave.*
ANATUPAPAKU: a burial cave at Waikereru Bay, Lake Okataina.

LEGENDS OF ROTORUA

AORANGI: a tributary of the Utuhina stream. Lit. *cloud in the sky.*
AORIKARIA: a point on the west shore of Lake Tarawera.
ARAWA: the park at Rotorua, named after the Arawa tribe.
ARIKIKAPAKAPA: (page 41) a lake and thermal area at the edge of Arikikapakapa Golf course, Rotorua. *Fluttering hot springs.*
ARIKIROA: (page 32) now known as the Postmaster Bath. *Long spring.*
ARTIST'S PALETTE: a formation at Orakei Korako.
ARATIATIA: rapids on the Waikato River, below the Huka Falls. Lit. *path of the ladder.*
ATAAHUA: a canyon and stream to the west of Lake Rotorua. Lit. *beautiful* or *pleasant.*
ATIAMURI: on the Waikato River, 28 miles south-west of Rotorua. Named after a local woman of high rank, believed to have been turned to stone.
AWAHOU: (pages 75-79) a village and stream on the west shore of Lake Rotorua. (Now Taniwha Springs.) See also Te Awahou. Lit. *new river.*

BLACK CRATER: Waimangu Valley. A descriptive name.
BLUE BATH: (pages 31-32) Rotorua. Maori name Oruawhata. Named from the colour of the water.
BLUE LAKE: (pages 128-133) 7 miles south-east of Rotorua, on the road to Lake Tarawera. Maori name Tikitapu. Named because of its colour.
BRAIN POT: (pages 38-39) a formation, once a geyser, at Whakarewarewa. The Maori name was Te Komutumutu. The brains of the chief Te Tukutuku were cooked in it.
BRIDAL VEIL FALLS: a formation below the Primrose Terrace at Waiotapu; also a similar formation at Wairakei.
BURIED VILLAGE: 10 miles south-east from Rotorua, near Lake Tarawera. The Maori name was Te Wairoa, and it was called by this name until the Tarawera eruption, when the village was buried in ash and mud.

CHAMPAGNE POOL: a large pool at Waiotapu, which bubbles like champagne if sand is thrown into it. There is another pool with similar properties at Whakarewarewa. The Champagne Pool or Cauldron at Wairakei is a collection of independent fountains.
CHERRY BAY: on the south shore of Lake Rotoiti.

DANCING ROCK: a rock weighing about ½ ton, which begins to sway before the Twins Geyser erupts at Wairakei.
DEVIL'S CAULDRON: a boiling pool at Tikitere.
DEVIL'S PORRIDGE POT: a mud pool at Tikitere.
DEVIL'S THROAT: at Orakei Korako. The Maori name was Te Korokoro o te Taipo, *the throat of the Devil.*
DRAGON'S MOUTH GEYSER: at Wairakei. The distinctive formation at the mouth of the geyser has led to its name.

PLACE NAMES OF THE THERMAL REGION

EAGLE'S NEST: a group of three geysers at Wairakei. It was named because of the petrified branches of trees which have the appearance of a nest.

EARTHQUAKE FLAT: 13 miles south-east of Rotorua, at the junction of the Waimangu Main Highway and the Rotorua-Taupo State Highway.

ECHO CRATER: Waimangu Valley.

EXPLOSION CRATER: at Waiotapu.

FAIRY CRATER: Waimangu Valley.

FAIRY SPRINGS: (page 80) 3 miles north-west of Rotorua, on the shore of Lake Rotorua. Known to the Maoris as Puna-a-Tuhoe.

FRYING PAN LAKE: Waimangu Valley. Named because of its thermal activity. It occupies the site of the former Frying Pan Flat.

GIBRALTAR CLIFF: on the shore of Frying Pan Lake.

GIBRALTAR ROCK: a formation on the shore of Lake Rotoiti.

GISBORNE POINT: on south shore of Lake Rotoiti.

GOLDEN FLEECE TERRACE: at Orakei Korako. A descriptive name.

GOLDEN SPRINGS: 27 miles south of Rotorua, midway between Rotorua and Taupo, just off the Rotorua-Taupo State Highway.

GREEN LAKE: (pages 134-135) 8 miles south-east of Rotorua, Maori name Rotokakahi. Named because of its colour. Also a small lake on the east shore of Lake Rotomahana, and another at Waiotapu.

HAMURANA SPRINGS: (pages 73-74) also the stream north of Lake Rotorua, 9 miles from Rotorua. Known to the Maoris as Kaikai-tahuna and Te Puna-i-Hangarua. Hamurana is the Maori form of the Biblical name *Smyrna*.

HANNAH BAY: between Hinemoa Point and Ngunguru Point on the east shore of Lake Rotorua.

HAPAHAPAIA: on south shore of Lake Tarawera. Lit. *passed over* or *gone by*.

HAPARANGI: a hill about 10 miles south of Rotorua, 2,257 ft.

HAPE-O-TOROA: (page 143) the steaming cliffs of Lake Rotomahana, and also the hill half a mile west of the lake, 1,894 ft.

HAROHARO: hill 3 miles south of Lake Rotoehu, 2,529 ft. Lit. *vault of heaven*.

HATUPATU'S ROCK: (page 115) on the Taupo-Putaruru State Highway. The rock with a cavity where Hatupatu hid from the bird-woman.

HAUMINGI: the southern arm of Lake Okataina.

HAUPARU: a bay on the south shore of Lake Rotoiti.

HAWAIKI: a bay on the south shore of Lake Tarawera. Hawaiki was the *homeland* of the Maoris.

HELL'S GATE: A popular name for Tikitere.

HEMO: A gorge on the road south from Rotorua, between Whakarewarewa and Atiamuri Junction. The sisters of Ngatoro climbed a hill between Lake Tarawera and Rotorua. One of them slipped when coming down and called the place Te Hemo, *to be faint*.

LEGENDS OF ROTORUA

HERDMAN'S BAY: on the west shore of Lake Rotoiti. Maori name Kakaho.

HIKATAUA: on the west shore of Lake Rotoma. Lit. *rites performed by a war party.*

HINEHOPU POINT: on the eastern shore of Lake Rotoiti. Named after Hinehopu.

HINEHOPU'S TREE: (pages 100-103) the wishing tree on Hongi's Track, between Lakes Rotoiti and Rotoehu, 18 miles from Rotorua.

HINEMOA POINT: at Owhata on the south-east shore of Lake Rotorua. This was the point of Hinemoa's departure from her village when she swam to Mokoia Island.

HINEMOA'S STEPS: at Okere Falls.

HINE-TUA-HOANGA: (pages 47-49) the sacred stone in the Wai-orotoki stream.

HONGI'S TRACK: (pages 57, 103-104) 18 miles from Rotorua, on the Rotorua-Whakatane Highway, between Lakes Rotoiti and Rotoehu. Named after the famous Ngapuhi warrior in memory of his exploit in bringing his canoes overland between the two lakes.

HOROHORO: flat-topped ramparts between Rotorua and Orakei Korako. Lit. *to be shattered.*

HOT WATER STREAM: on south shore of Lake Rotoiti.

HOPETETE: a point on the east shore of the Green lake.

HUITERANGIORA: a pa on west shore of Lake Rotoehu. *A famous legendary name.*

HUKA: on the Waikato River, 3 miles from Taupo. The name means *foam.*

HURITINI: boiling mud cauldron at Tikitere. *Ever-circling, the name of a woman of high rank.*

INDICATOR GEYSER: at Wairakei. It indicates when the Prince of Wales geyser is about to play.

INFERNO CRATER: Waimangu Valley.

INFERNO, THE: Tikitere.

INKPOT GEYSER: at Wairakei, named because of its sombre colour.

IODINE STREAM: Waimangu Valley.

IRIIRI-KAPUA: a rock at Owhata where Hinemoa listened to Tutanekai's flute.

KAIKAI-TAHUNA: (page 73) one of the Maori names of Hamurana Springs.

KAIKAKAHI: a bay on west shore of Lake Okataina. Lit. *a meal of fresh-water shell-fish.*

KAINGAROA PLAINS: (page 13) part of the volcanic plateau north and east of Lake Taupo. *The long meal,* a reference to the time taken by Haungaroa, sister of Ngatoro-i-rangi, in eating her meal.

KAITERIRIA: (page 135) at the southern extremity of the Green Lake.

KAITUNA: river which flows from Lake Rotoiti. Lit. *to eat eels* or *a feast of eels.*

PLACE NAMES OF THE THERMAL REGION

KAIWAKA: (page 143) a stream which connected Lakes Rotomahana and Tarawera before the eruption, also a place on the east shore of Lake Okataina. *To eat canoes*, a name given to turbulent rivers which were perilous for canoes.

KAKAHO: a bay on the west shore of Lake Rotoiti. Also known as Herdmans Bay. Lit. *culm of the toetoe*.

KAKANUI: (page 94) an old Maori village on Lake Rotoiti. Lit. *many parrots*.

KAPENGA: a swamp 7 miles south of Rotorua. Lit. *passed by* or *rejected*.

KARAKA: (page 80) the old-time pa on the summit of the hill above Fairy Springs. Lit. *name of a native tree*.

KARAPITI: (page 14) the famous blow-hole at Wairakei.

KARIRI: a point on the west shore of Lake Tarawera. Maori form of *Galilee*.

KAUAKA: a stream which flows beside the Rotorua-Taupo State Highway.

KAWAHA: (pages 44-46): a hilly peninsula and settlement on the west shore of Lake Rotorua, about two miles from Ohinemutu.

KAWA-TE-TANGI: (pages 60, 66) the site of Tutanekai's home on Mokoia Island.

KING'S HEAD: a boiling pool at Whakarewarewa.

KOA: a peak on Mount Tarawera, 3,360 ft.

KOMUTUMUTU: stream flowing into Lake Rotorua from the west, and also Maori name for The Brainpot, Whakarewarewa. Lit. *to cut off* or *truncate*. See under The Brainpot.

KOROKITEWAO: a bay on the east shore of Lake Rotoiti.

KOTARE: a hill four miles west of Lake Rotorua. Lit. *kingfisher*.

KOTORINOA: a point on the south shore of Lake Rotoiti.

KOTUKUTUKU: a bay on the west shore of Lake Tarawera. Lit. *fuchsia tree*.

KOURA-MAWHITIWHITI: (page 34) the foreshore of Lake Rotorua from the Government Grounds to the wharf. Lit. *crayfish struggling in the net*.

KOUTU: a settlement near Ohinemutu, and a bay on the west shore of Lake Rotoiti. Lit. *promontory*.

KUHARUA: (page 100) a point on the north shore of Lake Rotoiti. Lit. *shellfish in a pit*. Also known as Lees Point.

KUIRAU: the reserve at Rotorua. Lit. *many springs*.

LADY KNOX GEYSER: Waiotapu. Named after Lady Constance Knox, daughter of Lord Ranfurly, in 1896.

LEES POINT: on the north shore of Lake Rotoiti. Maori name Kuharua.

LEWIS HILL: to the east of Rotorua.

LOOKOUT ROCK: on the east shore of Lake Okataina.

LEGENDS OF ROTORUA

MAKETU: (pages 9, 13-14, 16, 122) on the Bay of Plenty Coast, at the mouth of the Kaituna River. The name is that of a kumara plantation in Hawaiki.

MALFROY GEYSERS: (page 31) artificial geysers constructed in the Government Grounds at Rotorua by J. M. C. Malfroy.

MAMAKU: 14 miles east of Rotorua, on the Rotorua Cambridge State Highway. *Tree fern.*

MANGAKAKAHI: a stream flowing into Lake Rotorua at Ohinemutu. Lit. *stream of fresh-water shellfish.*

MANGAKOTUKUTUKU: a tributary of the Tarawera River. Lit. *stream where the fuchsia tree grows.*

MANUPIRUA: hot springs on the south shore of Lake Rotoiti. Lit. *two small birds.*

MARAEROA: springs north of Tikitere. Lit. *long courtyard.*

MARAETAI: a point on the south shore of Lake Rotoiti.

MARAUA: a pa on the west shore of Lake Rotoehu. Lit. *name of fish.*

MARUWERA: a pa on the west shore of Lake Rotoehu.

MATAHI: a lagoon on the east shore of Lake Rotoma.

MATAU: on the east shore of Lake Rotoma. Lit. *fish-hook.*

MATAWHAO: a point on the west shore of Lake Rotoiti.

MATAWHAURA: (pages 68, 96) a mountain, 1,806 ft, on the east shore of Lake Rotoiti, and a bay on the west shore of Lake Rotoehu, two miles east of the mountain. Lit. *battle, warfare.*

MATUTU: on west shore of Lake Rotoma. Lit. *part of the figurehead of a canoe.*

MAUI: a small lake at the source of the Wairewarewa stream. The word has several meanings, and was also the name of the famous demi-god of Maori mythology.

MAUNGAKARAMEA: the Maori name for Rainbow Mountain. Lit. *mountain where the speargrass grows.*

MAUNGAONGAONGA: a mountain one mile west of Rainbow Mountain, 2,764 ft. Lit. *mountain where nettles grow.*

MAUNGAWHAKAMANA: a hill 3 miles south of Lake Rotoma. Lit. *mountain to give respect to.*

MIRROR LAKE: alongside the road to Lake Okataina.

MISSION BAY: on north shore of Lake Rotorua.

MOERANGI: (pages 81, 129-131) a hill one mile to west of the Blue Lake. Lit. *sleepy sky.*

MOKAI: a point on the north shore of Lake Rotoiti. Lit. *slave.*

MOKOIA: (pages 19, 32, 53-66, 69-70, 104, 110, 117-127) the island in Lake Rotorua. The name means *tattooed*, being a play on the words *moko* (tattooed) and *ko* (digging implement).

MOKOROA: point on the western shore of Lake Okataina. Lit. *a large white grub,* or an *atua* said to cause disease.

MOTUMAURI: an island in Lake Rotoiti. Lit. *island of the talisman.*

MOTUOHA: a point on the south shore of Lake Rotoiti. Lit. *island of greeting.*

PLACE NAMES OF THE THERMAL REGION

MOTUOHIWA: an island in Lake Rotoiti. Lit. *island of the steering paddle*, or *island belonging to Hiwa*.

MOTUTAIKO: (pages 15, 23) island at the south end of Lake Taupo. Lit. *island of the black petrel*.

MOTUTAPU-A-TINIRAU: (page 46) the original name given by Ihenga to Mokoia Island in Lake Rotorua. *The sacred island of Tinirau*.

MOTUTARA: a point in the Government Grounds, Rotorua, and the site of the Motutara Golf Course. Lit. *island of the gulls*.

MOTUTAWA: (pages 96-97, 135) an island in the Green Lake, where Hinemoa is buried. Also a peninsula on the south shore of Lake Rotoiti. Lit. *island of the tawa trees*.

MOTUWHETERO: an island in the western arm of Lake Okataina. Lit. *protruding island*.

MOURA: (page 137) a point on the south shore of Lake Tarawera, the site of one of the Maori villages which was buried in the Tarawera eruption.

MOUREA: (page 72) a point of land and a pa which once stood by the Ohau channel. *Remnant*.

MOU-TOHORA: (page 11) Maori name of Whale Island in the Bay of Plenty.

MURUIKA: (pages 21, 24) peninsula at Ohinemutu.

NEW RIVER: (pages 75-79) Te Awahou stream at Taniwha Springs. This is the Pakeha meaning of Awahou.

NGAHEWA: a small lake by the Rotorua-Taupo State Highway.

NGAIKI: a point on the north shore of Lake Rotoiti.

NGAKAHU: a point on the north shore of Lake Rotoiti. Lit. *the garments*.

NGAKORO: a small lake at Waiotapu.

NGAKUHU: a point on the north shore of Lake Rotoiti. Lit. *the cooking sheds*.

NGAPOURI: a small lake 2 miles west of Waiotapu.

NGAREHU: a peninsula on the south shore of Lake Rotoiti. Lit. *the mists*.

NGATAUTARA: a hill one mile south-west of Rotorua. Lit. *the hill tops*.

NGAURUHOE: (pages 11, 13) mountain between Tongariro and Ruapehu, 7,515 ft. Named after Ngatoro-i-rangi's slave Auruhoe.

NGAWHERO: a lake close to the south shore of Lake Rotoiti.

NGAWHIRA: hill at west end of Mount Tarawera.

NGONGOAHI: on north shore of Lake Rotoiti.

NGONGOTAHA: (pages 47, 81-86) village and mountain, 2,484 ft, on western shore of Lake Rotorua. *Funnel of the calabash*.

NGUNGURU: on east shore of Lake Rotorua. Lit. *to rumble or murmur*.

OHAU: (pages 43, 57, 72) channel connecting Lakes Rotorua and Rotoiti. *The place of Hau*, Ihenga's dog.

LEGENDS OF ROTORUA

OHINEMUTU: (pages 20-27) the Maori village at Rotorua. *The place of the girl cut off.*
OHINENUI: a tributary of the Ngongotaha stream. Lit. *the place of many girls.*
OHINETEKURA: on west shore of Lake Tarawera.
OHOUKAKA: (pages 93-96) a bay on Lake Rotoiti.
OHUANUI: a tributary of the Waiohewa stream. Lit. *place of many fruit.*
OKAHU: a point on the east shore of Lake Rotoehu. Lit. *the place of the hawk.*
OKAREKA: a lake one mile west of Lake Tarawera. Lit. *the place of sweet food.*
OKARO: a lake one mile south of Waimangu Valley.
OKATAINA: (pages 108-109) a lake between Lakes Rotorua, Rotoiti and Tarawera, 19 miles from Rotorua. *The place of laughter.*
OKAWA: a bay at the western end of Lake Rotoiti.
OKERE: (page 98) a stream entering Lake Rotoiti from the north; also falls on the river. An earlier name of the falls was Tutea. Lit. *the place of floating or drifting.*
OMAHOTA: an inlet on north shore of Lake Rotoehu.
OMARUPOTO: a bay on the north shore of Lake Rotoiti.
ONEPOTO: a bay on the north shore of Lake Rotoiti. Lit. *short beach.*
ONEROA: on the south-west shore of Lake Tarawera. Lit. *long beach.*
ONEWHERO: a lagoon on east shore of Lake Rotoma. Lit. *red beach.*
ONGURU: (page 98) the site of the singing tree near Kakanui on Lake Rotoiti. Lit. *to murmur.*
OPAL LAKE: 17 miles from Rotorua, off the Rotorua-Taupo State Highway.
OPAWHERO: a hill to the north of Rotorua Lake Tarawera Main Highway, one mile west of Lake Okareka, 1,620 ft.
ORAKEI KORAKO: (page 11) a thermal region on the Waikato River, 36 miles south of Rotorua. *The place of adorning.*
OREMU: a point on the north shore of Lake Rotoiti. Lit. *the place of tail-feathers.*
OROTU: a small lake at Waiotapu.
ORUAROA: a point on the south arm of Lake Okataina. Lit. *place of the two pits.*
ORUAWHATA: (pages 29-32) the chasm which is now the site of the Blue Bath. Lit. *place of the storehouse pit.*
OTANGIMOANA: the southern arm of Lake Okataina. Lit. *place of the sounding sea.*
OTANGIWAI: a point on the west shore of Lake Rotorua. Lit. *place of the sounding waters.*
OTARAMARAE: a point and bay on the north shore of Lake Rotoiti.
OTAUTAU: a bay on the east shore of Lake Rotoehu.
OTEI: springs on the west shore of Lake Rotoma. Lit. *place of the brown teal.*

PLACE NAMES OF THE THERMAL REGION

OTU-KAPUA-RANGI: (page 144) the boiling cauldron on top of the Pink Terraces. Lit. *cloud of heaven.*
OTUKAUAE: a point in Okawa Bay, Lake Rotoiti.
OTUMAROKURA: a hill on a peninsula on the north shore of Lake Rotoma, 1,190 ft, and a lagoon immediately to the west.
OTUMUTU: an island off the north shore of Lake Tarawera.
OTUROA: two miles north-west of Lake Rotorua.
OTUTANGAROA: a hill three miles to west of Lake Rotorua, 1,235 ft.
OTUTARARA: a hot spring north of Tikitere.
OWHATA: (pages 60, 67) a village on the shore of Lake Rotorua, five miles from Rotorua. Lit. *the place of the store-house.*
OWHITIKI: a point on the north shore of the Green Lake. Lit. *the place of a girdle.*

PADDLE WHEEL GEYSER: at Wairakei. It sounds like a paddle wheel steamer.
PAKARAKA: a rock 10 miles south of Rotorua, on the Rotorua-Taupo State Highway.
PAKARUAMARO: a mountain north of Lake Rotoiti.
PANGOPANGO: on the west shore of Lake Rotoma.
PAPA-I-OURU: the marae at Ohinemutu.
PAPAKARARO: a rock off the west shore of Lake Rotoiti.
PAPAKURA: (page 39) a geyser at Whakarewarewa. Lit. *red earth.*
PAPA-NGAEHEEHE: (page 41) near Arikikapakapa, Rotorua. Lit. *rocky flat of rustling sounds.*
PAPAROA: rock and reef on the west shore of Lake Rotoiti. Lit. *long flat.*
PARADISE VALLEY SPRINGS: on Clayton Road, 4 miles west of Rotorua.
PARANGIIA: a hill on the north shore of Lake Rotoiti.
PARENGARENGA: hot springs on a point on the south shore of Lake Rotoiti. Lit. *leggings made of flax leaves.*
PARETEIRO: a hill at Tikitere, 1,290 ft.
PAREURU: (pages 110, 117) a pass between Rotorua and the Buried Village.
PAREWHAITI: a hill near the Buried Village, 1,741 ft.
PARIKAWAU: a point on the north shore of Lake Rotoiti. Lit. *shag cliff.*
PARIMATA: a bay on the west shore of Lake Okataina.
PATARATA: a point on the east shore of Lake Rotoma.
PATEKO: (page 98) an island on Lake Rotoiti. Lit. *motionless.*
PEREREMU: a hill 3 miles north-west of Lake Rotorua, 1,455 ft.
PICNIC POINT: (page 32) in Government Grounds, Rotorua. The Maori name was Te Toto.
PIHANGA: a mountain south of Tokaanu above Lake Rotoaira, 4,352 ft. Lit. *window.*
PINK TERRACES: (pages 136, 143) before their destruction by the eruption of Tarawera the Pink Terraces rose above Lake Rotomahana. Named because of their colour.

LEGENDS OF ROTORUA

POHATUROA: (page 35) a mountain, 1,420 ft, near Whakarewarewa; also the distinctive rock one mile south-west of Atiamuri, 1,705 ft. Lit. *the tall rock.*

POHUE: a settlement on the east shore of Lake Rotorua. Lit. *a plant resembling the convolvulus.*

POHUTU: (page 39) the famous geyser at Whakarewarewa. Lit. *to splash.*

PONGAKAWA: (pages 57, 103) a stream which rises in Lake Rotoehu. Lit. *to consume.*

POSTMASTER BATH: (page 32) in Government Grounds, Rotorua. Maori name Arikiroa.

POTAKA: 2 miles north-west of Lake Rotorua. Lit. *a top.*

POTANGATANGA: a point on the north shore of Lake Rotoiti.

POTANGOTANGO: a point on the south shore of Lake Rotoiti.

PRIEST'S BATH: (pages 31-32) at the Government Spa, Rotorua. The Maori name was Te Pupunitanga. Named after Father Mahoney. Its waters feed the Ward Baths.

PRIMROSE TERRACE: a formation at Waiotapu which is mainly yellow in colour.

PRINCE OF WALES FEATHERS: a boiling pool at Whakarewarewa which erupts on occasion. It divides into two or three plumes.

PUARENGA: (page 40) the stream which flows through Whakarewarewa to Lake Rotorua. It is a name with several meanings: pua, *flower;* renga, *overflowing, discoloured, yellow,* or *pollen.*

PUHIRUA: a pa on north shore of Lake Rotorua.

PUKEHOU: on south shore of Lake Tarawera. Lit. *new hill.*

PUKEMOTITI: a bay on the north shore of Lake Rotoiti.

PUKENUI: a hill on the south shore of Lake Rotoiti, 1,350 ft. Lit. *big hill.*

PUKEPOTO: a hill between Lakes Rotorua and Okataina, 2,250 ft. Lit. *short hill.*

PUKEROA: (page 28) hill and park in Rotorua. Lit. *long hill.*

PUKETAPU: a point on the north shore of Lake Rotoiti. Lit. *sacred hill.*

PUKETITOI: a point on the south shore of Lake Rotoiti. Lit. *mocking hill.*

PUKURAHI: (page 59) a pa on Mokoia Island. Lit. *big stomach.*

PUNA-A-TUHOE: (page 80) the spring now known as Fairy Springs. *The spring of Tuhoe* (ancestor of the Tuhoe tribe).

PUNARUKU: an island in the western arm of the Green Lake. Lit. *to sink into the spring.*

PUNAWHAKAREIA: on the south shore of Lake Rotoiti. Lit. *to throw into the spring.*

PUREHUREHU: on the south shore of Lake Rotoma. Lit. *small patches of mist.*

PURURU: a hill, 2,105 ft, one mile north of Mount Ngongotaha. Lit. *shady,* or *thick with the leaves.*

PURUTOETOE: a point on the west shore of Lake Rotoehu. Lit. *to plug with toetoe grass.*

PLACE NAMES OF THE THERMAL REGION

PUTAUAKI: a point on the west shore of Lake Tarawera.
PUTUATUA: a pa on the west shore of Lake Rotoehu.

RACHEL BATH: (page 32) in the Government Spa, Rotorua. The Maori name was Whangapipiro. Its waters feed the Ward Baths.
RADIUM BATH: also feeds the Ward Baths.
RAHUIROA: on the western arm of Lake Tarawera. Lit. *the long bundle.*
RAINBOW FALLS: on the Waikato River between Rotorua and Atiamuri. Named because of their appearance.
RAINBOW MOUNTAIN: 18 miles south of Rotorua by the Rotorua-Taupo State Highway. Named because of its coloured rocks of many hues. Maori name Maungakaramea.
RAINBOW TERRACE: at Orakei Korako.
RAKAUMAKERE: on the south shore of Lake Rotoehu. Lit. *fallen timber.*
RANGIURU: on the western shore of Lake Tarawera. Lit. *the western sky.*
RAPATU: on the south shore of Lake Tarawera.
REREWHAKAITU: a lake 3 miles south-east of Lake Rotomahana. Lit. *to flow aside.*
RIVER CAVE: at Okere Falls.
ROCKY POINT: in the Government Grounds, Rotorua.
ROTOAIRA: (pages 22-23) a lake between Mounts Tongariro and Pihanga. *Lake of Ira.*
ROTOATUA: a small lake near Mirror Lake on the Okataina Road. Lit. *Lake of the god.*
ROTOEHU: (pages 11, 57, 103, 105-106, 129) a lake between Lakes Rotoiti and Rotoma. Lit. *turbid lake.*
ROTOITI: (pages 11, 17, 43, 57, 92-104, 106, 121) a lake 14 miles from Rotorua, between Lakes Rotorua and Rotoma. It is connected by the Ohau Channel to Lake Rotorua. *The little lake.*
ROTOKAKAHI: (pages 134-135) the Maori name of the Green Lake. *Lake of the fresh-water mussel.*
ROTOKAWA: a small lake and settlement near the east shore of Lake Rotorua, about six miles from Rotorua. *Bitter lake.*
ROTOKAWAU: (pages 89-91) a lake about one mile from Tikitere, about 11 miles from Rotorua. *Shag lake.*
ROTOMA: (page 105) a lake to the east of Lake Rotoehu, 23 miles from Rotorua. *Clear lake.*
ROTOMAHANA: (pages 136, 141, 143-144) a lake one mile south of Lake Tarawera, about 18 miles from Rotorua. *Warm lake.*
ROTONGATA: a small lake two miles south of Lake Rotoiti. Lit. *tiny lake.*
ROTORUA: (pages 11, 19, 20, 43-52, 70) the largest lake of the thermal regions, the name later being given to the town (pages 23-34, 43). *The second lake.*
ROTOWHERO: a small lake on the Rotorua-Taupo State Highway, 2¼ miles south of Waimangu Valley. Lit. *red lake.*

LEGENDS OF ROTORUA

ROTOWHIO: (page 41) a small lake at Whakarewarewa, which has also given its name to the model pa. Lit. *lake of the blue duck*.
RUAHINE: spring on the south shore of Lake Rotoiti. Lit. *wise woman*.
RUAPEKA: (pages 21, 24) a bay at Ohinemutu. At one time the pa at this village was known as Ruapeka pa. Lit. *fern-root pit*.
RUATO: on the south shore of Lake Rotorua.
RUAWAHIA: (page 140) a peak on Mount Tarawera, 3,646 ft. Lit. *pit broken into*, or *broken in two places*.

SATAN'S BOILING KETTLE OF DOUGH: Tikitere.
SATAN'S CLARET CUP: Tikitere.
SATAN'S GLORY: Tikitere.
SATAN'S MIXING TROUGH: Tikitere.
SODOM AND GOMORRAH: a sulphurous area near Arikikapakapa, Rotorua, named after the Biblical cities near the Dead Sea which were destroyed by fire and brimstone.
SOUTHERN CRATER: Waimangu Valley.
SULPHUR POINT: at Government Grounds, Rotorua. A descriptive name.

TAHUNA (pages 103, 106) the pass traversed by Hongi's canoes, and therefore the Maori name for Hongi's Track. Lit. *sandbank* or *shoal*.
TAHUNAPO: on the north shore of Lake Okataina. Lit. *sandbank by night*.
TAHUNAROA: a point on the south shore of Lake Rotoiti. Lit. *long sandbank*.
TAKIWA-WAIARIKI: the Maori name for the thermal region. *District of the hot springs*.
TAMATEKAPUA: the meeting house at Ohinemutu, named after the captain of the Arawa canoe.
TANGATARUA: a hill one mile to the west of Whakarewarewa. Lit. *two men*.
TANIWHA: (pages 74-79) springs on west side of Lake Rotorua, and 8 miles from Rotorua; also a rock (page 140) which at one time was to be seen at Lake Tarawera. *Monster*.
TAPANIAU: a point on the south shore of Lake Rotoiti.
TAPAPAKURU: a tributary of the Waiteti stream. Lit. *to pound flat*.
TAPUAEHARURU: (pages 96, 104) an ancient pa on the east shore of Lake Rotoiti. *Resounding footsteps*.
TAPUAEKURA: (page 92) a bay on the south shore of Lake Rotoiti. Lit. *footsteps of a chief*.
TAR AND PITCH POT: Tikitere.
TARAPATIKI: on the west shore of Lake Tarawera.
TARAWERA: (pages 11, 136-143) the lake and the mountain, 3,770 ft, 10 to 15 miles south-east of Rotorua. *Burnt spears*.
TAREWA: an old Maori village amongst the hot springs near the Kuirau thermal area at Rotorua. The name in full is Tarewa-pounamu, *to suspend a greenstone ornament*.

PLACE NAMES OF THE THERMAL REGION

TARUKENGA: a settlement on the Rotorua Branch Railway, 4 miles west of Lake Rotorua. Lit. *slaughter*.

TAUHARA: (page 13) a mountain, 3,603 ft, on pumice plains between Taupo and the Kaingaroa Plains. The central trig station of the North Island. Lit. *isolated, standing alone*.

TAUHERE-RAU-TI: (page 34) a place near Picnic Point, Government Grounds, Rotorua. Lit. *bird-snare made of cabbage tree leaves*.

TAUPO: (pages 10, 11, 13, 14, 23) the largest lake in the centre of the North Island. *A black and yellow cloak*.

TAURANGA: a town 54 miles north of Rotorua on the Bay of Plenty. Lit. *canoe anchorage*.

TAURANGANUI: a bay on the north shore of Lake Okataina; also on the north-west corner of the Green Lake. Lit. *big canoe anchorage*.

TAWHITINUI: a hill at Ngarehu Point, Lake Rotoiti. Lit. *big snare*.

TE AHAU: on the south shore of Lake Rotoehu. Lit. *the temporary break-wind for crops*.

TE AHI-MANAWA: (page 128) the ridge between the Blue and Green Lakes. *The fire where the heart was cooked*. The name in full is one of the longest in Maoridom—Te tuahu a Tuameke te ahi tapoa; taona ai te manawa o Taiapua, which means *The sacred place of Tuameke, the fire of witchcraft incantation in which the heart of Taiapua was cooked*.

TE AKAU: a point on the north shore of Lake Rotoiti. Lit. *the reef*.

TE ANA-O-WAITAPU: (page 34) a cave on a small island near Picnic Point, Rotorua. *The cave of Waitapu*.

TE ARERO: a bay on the north shore of Lake Rotoiti. Lit. *the tongue*.

TE ARIKI: (pages 137, 141) a Maori village on the south shore of Lake Tarawera, destroyed in the eruption of 1886. Lit. *the chief*.

TE AWAHOU: (pages 75-79) the river at Taniwha Springs. *The new river*.

TE HAEHAENGA: a hill 5 miles south of Lake Rotoehu, 1,045 ft. Lit. *cut up* or *lacerated*.

TE HAPUA: a lake close to the north shore of Lake Rotoiti. Lit. *the pool* or *lagoon*.

TE HINAU: (page 39) an alkaline spring at Whakarewarewa. Lit. *the hinau* (tree).

TE HIRAU: a bay on the south shore of Lake Tarawera. Lit. *the paddle*.

TE HIWI-O-TE-TOROA: (pages 51-52) water heaped above a shoal in Lake Rotorua, stretching from Owhata to Kawaha. *The ridge of the albatross*.

TE HORO: a boiling spring at Whakarewarewa which erupts on occasion. Lit. *the spring*.

TE KAINGA: a bay on the west shore of Lake Rotoiti. Lit. *the village*.

TE KARAKA: a bay on the north shore of Lake Rotoiti. Lit. *the karaka* (tree).

TE KARAMEA: a bay on the west shore of Lake Tarawera. Lit. *the spear-grass*.

Baptism scene

TE KAUAE: (page 84) a steep precipice on Mount Ngongotaha. *The jaw.*
TE KAUANGA-A-HATUPATU: (page 32) a village by the shore of Lake Rotorua, now deserted. *The swimming of Hatupatu.*
TE KERAU: a bay on the north shore of Lake Rotoiti.
TE KOMUTUMUTU: (page 39) a formation at Whakarewarewa, once a geyser, but now quiescent. Modern name The Brainpot. *The calabash with the top cut off.*
TE KOROKORO O TE TAIPO: Maori name of the Devil's Throat, Orakei Korako.
TE KOUTU: (page 108) an island or peninsula on Lake Okataina. Lit. *promontory.*
TE KUMETE: a hill one mile south of Lake Tarawera, 1,830 ft. Lit. *the wooden bowl.*
TE MAMAKU: a point on the north shore of Lake Rotoiti. Lit. *the tree fern.*
TE MATUA-TONGA: (page 56) a sacred stone kumara god on Mokoia Island.
TE MAURI-OHORERE-A-HATUPATU: (page 50) a long white rock on the bed of Lake Rotorua, midway between Sulphur Point and Mokoia Island. *The startled soul of Hatupatu.*

TE MIRO: a point on the west shore of Lake Tarawera. Lit. *The miro* (tree).

TE MOANA-NUI-A-KAHU: (page 47) an early name for Lake Rotorua. *The big sea of Kahu.*

TE MOKOROA: a point on the north shore of Lake Rotoiti. Lit. *the long lizard.*

TE MOTUTAPU: (page 27) an island close to Ohinemutu.

TE MOTU-TAPU-A-IHENGA: (page 47) a grove of trees by the Wai-oro-toki stream. *The sacred grove of Ihenga.*

TE MOTU-TAPU-A-TINIRAU (pages 19, 54) an early name for Mokoia Island

TE NGAE: (pages 67-72, 88) a village on the east shore of Lake Rotorua. *The swamp.*

TE ONEPOTO: on the west shore of Lake Rotoma. Lit. *the short beach.*

TE PAEPAE-HAKUMANU: (page 34) a place near Picnic Point, Government Grounds, Rotorua. Lit. *the place of bird-snares.*

TE PAPA-O-TE-ARAWA: (page 34) a flat rock near Picnic Point, Rotorua. Lit. *the rock of the Arawa.*

TE PAPATU: a point on the north shore of Lake Rotoiti. Lit. *the screen used for defensive purposes.*

TE PARE-A-HATUPATU: (pages 56) a totara tree and also a grove of trees on Mokoia Island. *The head-wreath of Hatupatu.*

TE PERA-O-TANGAROA (pages 44-46) a tuahu (altar) at Kawaha, on the shore of Lake Rotorua. Lit. *the putrefying flesh.*

TE POHOE: a point on the north shore of Lake Rotoiti.

TE POHUE: a bay on the south-west corner of Lake Rotoehu. Lit. *the pohue* (climbing plant).

TE PUAPUA: a point on the south shore of Lake Rotoiti. Lit. *the present.*

TE PUIA: (pages 35-36) a pa situated on a hill which bears the same name, above Whakarewarewa. Lit. *the spring.*

TE PUNA: a bay on the west shore of the Green Lake. Lit. *the spring.*

TE PUNA-A-TUHOE: the Maori name for Fairy Springs. *The spring of Tuhoe.*

TE PUNA-I-HANGARUA: (page 73) one of the Maori names for Hamurana Springs. *The spring of Hangarua.*

TE PUPUNITANGA: (pages 31-32) a hot spring now known as the Priest's Bath. Lit. *the ambush.*

TE PUROKU: a point on the south-west shore of Lake Tarawera.

TE RATA: on the south shore of Lake Tarawera. Lit. *the rata* (tree).

TE REI: a bay on the south shore of Lake Rotoiti. Lit. *the cherished possession.*

TE REINGA: a tributary of the Utuhina stream. Lit. *the place of leaping.*

TE RORO-O-TE-RANGI: (page 32) steam which rises from Arikiroa the Postmaster Bath). Lit. *the brains of the sky.*

TE ROTORONUI: a small lake between Lakes Rotoiti and Tarawera.

Te Toto, "The Place of Blood", now more happily known as Picnic Point (see Chapter Four)

TE RUAKI-O-TE-KURI-A-IHENGA: (page 93) on the shore of Lake Rotoiti. *The vomit of Ihenga's dog.*
TE TAHEKE: a mountain north of Lake Rotoiti, 1,263 ft. Lit. *the steep descent.*
TE TAKAPOUOTERANGI ANIWHANIWHA: a place close to the west shore of the Blue Lake.
TE TAPAHORO: the north-east corner of Lake Tarawera. Lit. *the landslide on the margin.*
TE TAWA: a point on the south shore of Lake Okataina. Lit. *the tawa* (tree).
TE TI: a bay on the north shore of Lake Rotoiti. Lit. *the cabbage tree.*
TE TOHU: a point on the western arm of the Green Lake. Lit. *the division of an army.*
TE TORO: a stream flowing into Lake Rotorua from the south. Lit. *the toro* (tree).
TE TOROA: a point on the western shore of Lake Tarawera. Lit. *the albatross.*
TE TOTO: (page 32) the Maori name for Picnic point. *The blood, or the place of blood.*
TE TUAHU-O-TE-ATUA: (page 81) on the summit of Mount Ngongotaha. *The altar of the gods.*

160

PLACE NAMES OF THE THERMAL REGION

TE WAIROA: (pages 136-139) the Maori name of the Buried Village, near Lake Tarawera. Lit. *the long stream.*

TE WARO URI: (page 75) the Maori name for Taniwha Springs; the source of the Awahou River. *The dark chasm.*

TE WETA: a bay on the north shore of Lake Rotoiti. Lit. *the weta* (insect).

TE WHARE: a point on the west shore of Lake Tarawera. Lit. *the house.*

TE WHEKAU: a lagoon between Lakes Tarawera and Okareka. Lit. *the laughing owl.*

TIKITAPU: (pages 31, 47, 128-133) the Maori name for the Blue Lake between Lakes Rotorua and Tarawera. *The sacred tiki.*

TIKITERE: (pages 67, 68, 87-91) the thermal region 10 miles from Rotorua, south of Lake Rotoiti. The meaning of the full name of this place is: *our greatly loved daughter has floated away.*

TIKITIKI: a peninsula on the west shore of Lake Okataina. Lit. *girdle* or *topknot.*

TIKORANGI: a hill ½ mile north of Lake Rotorua, 1,514 ft.

TIRITIRI-MATANGI: (page 29) on old kumara plantation on the site of Arawa Street, Rotorua. *Twigs on the kumara mounds in the north-east breeze.*

TOKAANU: (page 23) hot springs resort at southern end of Lake Taupo.

TONGARIRO: (pages 10, 11) a mountain south of Lake Taupo, 6,458 ft. *Carried away by the south wind.*

TUARAE: on the south shore of Lake Rotoiti.

TUARA-HIWI-ROA: a place on the shore of Lake Rotorua. Lit. *long black ridge.*

TUKUTUKU: (page 39) a cave at Whakarewarewa, named after the chief Te Tukutuku.

TUMOANA: a peninsula on the south shore of Lake Rotoiti. Lit. *standing in the sea* (lake).

TURANGAORAKEIAO: a hill on the south shore of Lake Rotoiti.

TUTAEHEKA: a hill two miles south of Green Lake, 2,360 ft. Lit. *mouldy excrement.*

TUTEA: (page 98) an earlier name for Okere Falls. Named after a chief who lived there.

TWINS GEYSER: a double geyser at Wairakei.

UMURUA: a tributary of the Ngongotaha stream. Lit. *two ovens.*
UREKOHUA: a mountain north of Lake Rotorua, 1,577 ft.
UTUHINA: a stream which flows through Ohinemutu into Lake Rotorua.

VENUS BATH: Waiotapu.

WAHANGA: a peak on Mount Tarawera. Lit. *broken* or *split.*
WAIARIKI: a Maori name for a hot pool or spring.

LEGENDS OF ROTORUA

WAIHARURU: (page 42) a waterfall on Alum Creek, Rotorua. Lit. *rumbling waters.*

WAIHUAHUAKAKAHI: a tributary of the Puarenga stream. Lit. *the water in which the shellfish were boiled.*

WAIITI: a Maori school on the east shore of Lake Rotoiti. Lit. *little stream.*

WAIKAKAREAO: the eastern peak of Mount Tarawera.

WAIKARURU: a tributary of the Puarenga stream.

WAIKERERU: a bay on the east shore of Lake Okataina. Lit. *stream of the wood pigeon.*

WAI-KIMIHIA: (pages 60, 62-66) the warm pool on Mokoia Island, usually known as Hinemoa's Pool. Lit. *water searched for.*

WAIKITE: (page 38) a once famous geyser, now almost extinct, at Whakarewarewa. Lit. *water seen from afar.*

WAIMANGEAO: (page 41) the stream which drains Arikikapakapa, Rotorua, now known as Alum Creek. Lit. *pungent waters.*

WAIMANGU: the thermal valley between Lake Tarawera and the Rotorua-Taupo State Highway, 16 miles from Rotorua. Lit. *black water.*

WAIMATA: a stream entering Lake Rotokawau from the south.

WAIMEHIA: on the west shore of Lake Rotorua.

WAINGAEHE: a stream flowing north-east into Lake Rotorua. Lit. *rustling stream.*

WAINGARIRI: a tributary of the Okere River. Lit. *stream of love.*

WAIOHEWA: a stream running into Lake Rotorua from Tikitere.

WAIOHIRO: (page 44) a village near Ohinemutu. Lit. *stream of Whiro* (the god evil).

WAIONE: on the west shore of Lake Rotoehu. Lit. *stream on the beach.*

WAI-ORO-TOKI: (pages 47-49) a tributary of the Waiteti stream. *Adze sharpening water.*

WAIOTAPU: the thermal area 18½ miles south-east of Rotorua, east of the Rotorua-Taupo State Highway. Lit. *place of sacred waters.*

WAIOTEPAORA: a hill ¼ mile north of Mission Bay, Lake Rotorua.

WAIOTOKOMANGA: a tributary of the Puarenga stream. Lit. *place of the forked stream.*

WAIOWHIRO: a stream feeding Lake Rotorua north of Kawaha Point. See Waiohiro.

WAIOTEPAORA: half a mile south of Lake Rotorua.

WAIPA: a tributary of the Puarenga stream. Lit. *stream by the pa.*

WAIPUIA: a point on the east shore of Lake Rotoehu. Lit. *water of the springs.*

WAIPUNA: a bay on the east shore of Lake Rotoiti. Lit. *spring water.*

WAIRAKEI: thermal region near Taupo. Lit. *water of adorning.*

WAIRAU: a bay on the south shore of Lake Rotoiti. Lit. *many waters.*

WAIRERE: falls on the Wairoa stream near the Buried Village. Lit. *leaping water.*

PLACE NAMES OF THE THERMAL REGION

WAIREWAREWA: a tributary of the Waiohewa stream. Lit. *stream of the rewarewa* (tree).

WAIROA: see Te Wairoa; also the stream flowing through the Buried Village to Lake Tarawera. Lit. *long stream*.

WAIRUA: a stream flowing north to Lake Tarawera, also a hill half a mile north of Waimangu Valley, 1,961 ft. Lit. *two streams*.

WAITANGI: springs half a mile south of Lake Rotoehu, also a bay on the west shore of Lake Tarawera. Lit. *sounding waters*.

WAITETI: (page 47) a stream north of Ngongotaha on the west shore of Lake Rotorua. Lit. *stream of the cabbage tree*.

WAIWHERO: a tributary of the Waiteti stream. Lit. *red water or stream*.

WARBRICK GEYSER and TERRACES: Waimangu Valley. Named after the famous Maori guide, Alfred Warbrick.

WARD BATHS: at the Government Spa, Rotorua.

WERIWERI: ruins of a kainga, now seen only faintly, on the bank of Waiteti stream, Ngongotaha. Lit. *disgusting* or *provoked*.

WHAKAARI: Maori name for White Island, Bay of Plenty. Lit. *to show*.

WHAKAPOUNGAKAU: (page 89) a mountain between Lakes Okataina and Rotokawau, 2,490 ft. Lit. *the firmly established heart*, or *the hills of longing*.

WHAKAREWAREWA: (pages 35-42, 117) the Rotorua thermal sightseeing area. The name in full means *the leaping up of the army of Wahiao;* also a lagoon on the east shore of Lake Rotoma.

WHANGAMARINO: a Maori school on the north shore of Lake Rotoiti. Lit. *peaceful harbour*.

WHANGAMOA: a point on the north shore of Lake Rotoiti.

WHANGAPIPIRO: (page 32) the Maori name of Rachel Bath, the name being given because of its smell.

WHANGAROA: an inlet on the west shore of Lake Rotoma.

WHARETATA: a bay on the south shore of Lake Rotoiti.

WHENUAKURA: on the south shore of Lake Rotoiti. Lit. *red land*.

WHIOWHIO: a point on the north shore of Lake Rotoiti.

WHITE ISLAND: (pages 11, 14) a volcanic island in the Bay of Plenty. Maori name Whakaari.

WHITE TERRACES: (page 136) a formation at Lake Rotomahana, destroyed in the Tarawera eruption. Named because of their colour.

WISHING POOL: a pool at the foot of Aladdin's Cave, Orakei Korako.

WISHING TREE: on Hongi's Track, between Lakes Rotoiti and Rotoehu. The proper name is Hinehopu's Tree.